The Collection of the Exhibition of
Underwater Archaeology in China

水下考古在中国
专题陈列图录

宁波市文物考古研究所
编著　　宁波中国港口博物馆
国家文物局水下文化遗产保护中心

宁波出版社

编辑委员会

主　　任	赵惠峰　　柴晓明
副 主 任	舒月明　　徐建成　　王结华　　姜　波
主　　编	王结华
执行主编	王力军
副 主 编	冯　毅　　林国聪　　俞立禾
编　　务	王光远　　金　涛　　史　伟　　侯鲜婷
摄　　影	冯　毅　　孙　臣　　黄　欢　　李朱佳
翻　　译	周昳恒　　洪　欣

Compilation Institutes

Ningbo Municipal Institute of Cultural Relics and Archaeology

China Port Museum

National Center of Underwater Cultural Heritage

Editorial Committee

Directors: Zhao Huifeng　Chai Xiaoming

Deputy Directors: Shu Yueming　Xu Jiancheng　Wang Jiehua　Jiang Bo

Chief Editor: Wang Jiehua

Executive Chief Editor: Wang Lijun

Associate Chief Editors: Feng Yi　Lin Guocong　Yu Lihe

Editors: Wang Guangyuan　Jin Tao　Shi Wei　Hou Xianting

Photographers: Feng Yi　Sun Chen　Huang Huan　Li Zhujia

Translators: Zhou Yiheng　Hong Xin

目录 Contents

概　述 1

篇章一　展陈框架

前　言 20
机构与队伍 22
技术与方法 24
调查与发掘 26
保护与交流 28
规划与展望 30

篇章二　展陈文物

"南海Ⅰ号"南宋沉船 34
　龙泉窑青釉划花碗 36
　闽清义窑青白釉划花碗 37
　景德镇窑青白釉婴戏纹碗 38
　景德镇窑青白釉印花葵口碟 39
　磁灶窑绿釉印花碟 40
　磁灶窑酱釉扁罐 41
　磁灶窑酱釉四系罐 42

德化窑青白釉印花双系罐 …… 43
德化窑青白釉葫芦瓶 …… 44
德化窑青白釉印花喇叭口瓶 …… 45
德化窑青白釉粉盒 …… 46
铜环 …… 47

"半洋礁 I 号"南宋沉船 …… 48

福清东张窑黑釉兔毫盏 …… 50
福清东张窑黑釉盏 …… 52
福建青白釉花卉纹芒口碗 …… 54
福建青白釉花卉双鱼纹芒口碗 …… 55
福建青白釉婴戏纹芒口碗 …… 56
福清东张窑褐釉草叶纹盆 …… 57

绥中三道岗元代沉船 …… 58

磁州窑白釉褐彩鱼藻纹盆 …… 60
磁州窑白釉褐彩花草纹罐 …… 61
磁州窑白釉褐彩龙凤纹罐 …… 62
磁州窑黑白釉草叶纹碗 …… 64
磁州窑黑白釉草叶纹碗 …… 65
磁州窑黑白釉碗 …… 66
磁州窑黑釉菊瓣纹碗 …… 67
磁州窑黑釉菊瓣纹碗 …… 68
磁州窑白釉褐彩草叶纹器盖 …… 70
磁州窑白釉褐彩螺旋纹器盖 …… 71
磁州窑白釉褐彩草叶纹碟 …… 72
磁州窑白釉褐彩草叶纹碟 …… 73
磁州窑白釉褐彩草叶纹碟 …… 74
磁州窑白釉褐彩草叶纹碟 …… 75
磁州窑白釉梅瓶 …… 76

"南澳Ⅰ号"明代沉船 ……… 78

- 景德镇青花弦纹碗 ……… 80
- 景德镇青花弦纹碗 ……… 81
- 景德镇青花海水鱼龙纹碗 ……… 82
- 景德镇青花海水鱼龙纹碗 ……… 83
- 景德镇青花法螺应龙纹大碗 ……… 84
- 景德镇青花缠枝花卉开光葡萄纹大碗 ……… 85
- 景德镇青花高士图"福"款杯 ……… 86
- 景德镇青花高士图"福"款杯 ……… 87
- 景德镇青花花鸟纹杯 ……… 88
- 景德镇青花兰花纹杯 ……… 89
- 景德镇青花缠枝牡丹纹"福"款杯 ……… 90
- 景德镇青花折枝花卉纹"福"款杯 ……… 91
- 景德镇青花丹凤朝阳图盘 ……… 92
- 景德镇青花树石栏杆纹盘 ……… 93
- 景德镇青花树石栏杆纹盘 ……… 94
- 漳州窑青花菊花纹盘 ……… 95
- 漳州窑青花麒麟纹折沿盘 ……… 96
- 漳州窑青花缠枝花卉纹玉壶春瓶 ……… 97
- 漳州窑青花菊花纹碟 ……… 98
- 漳州窑青花菊花纹碟 ……… 99
- 漳州窑青花缠枝花卉纹小罐 ……… 100
- 漳州窑青花缠枝花卉纹小罐 ……… 101
- 漳州窑青花缠枝花卉纹净瓶 ……… 102
- 景德镇五彩玉兔四开光花卉纹粉盒 ……… 104

"碗礁Ⅰ号"清代沉船 ……… 106

- 景德镇青花婴戏碗 ……… 108
- 景德镇青花山水碗 ……… 109
- 景德镇青花山水碗 ……… 110

景德镇青花花卉碗	111
景德镇青花五开光折枝花卉盘	112
景德镇青花凤穿牡丹碟	113
景德镇青花团菊盘	114
景德镇青花十六开光五团菊菱口盘	116
景德镇青花十六开光洞石花卉菱口盘	118
景德镇青花蓝底冰梅盘	120
景德镇青花釉里红梅竹盘	122
景德镇青花高足杯	124
景德镇青花菊花深腹杯	125
景德镇五彩杂宝博古盘	126
景德镇五彩八开光折枝花博古盘	128

"小白礁I号"清代沉船 …… 130

景德镇"嘉庆"款青花缠枝花卉纹碗	132
景德镇"道光"款青花缠枝花卉纹碗	134
景德镇青花缠枝花卉纹碗	135
景德镇青花花草纹菱口豆	136
景德镇青花花草纹菱口豆	138
景德镇青花灵芝纹盘	140
景德镇青花菊瓣纹"福"款盘	142
景德镇青花花卉纹碟	143
景德镇青花缠枝花草纹灯盏	144
景德镇青花花卉纹杯	146
景德镇青花花草纹勺	147
景德镇五彩盖罐	148
紫砂壶	150
紫砂罐	151
酱釉陶壶	152

"源合盛记"印章	153
西班牙银币	154
测深铅锤	155

中山舰 ... 156

"中山"木牌	158
驳壳手枪	159
七九式步枪	160
七九式步枪刺刀	161
扳手	162
炮弹壳	163
弹壳笔筒	164
砚台	165
开信刀	166
中山军舰电报稿	167
铜纽扣	168
刮胡刀	169
军用水壶	170
"汉口赞誉"汽水瓶	171
"机舱"双耳搪瓷缸	172
"平海"搪瓷脸盆	173
手电筒	174
壁式可转动挂衣杆	175
手提灯	176

后 记 ... 178

Contents

Introduction 1

Chapter 1 Exhibition Outline

Preface ·· 20

Institutes and Staff ·· 22

Techniques and Methodologies ··· 24

Surveys and Excavations ··· 26

Preservation and Communication ··· 28

Plans and Expectations ··· 30

Chapter 2 Exhibition Artefacts

Southern Song Dynasty Shipwreck "Nanhai I" ·· 34

Longquan Kiln Celadon Bowl Incised with Floral Design 36

Fujian Qingyi Kiln Blue and White Glazed Bowl Incised with Floral Design 37

Jingdezhen Kiln Blue and White Glazed Bowl with Children Playing Design 38

Jingdezhen Kiln Blue and White Glazed Dish with Floral Petal-shaped Rim Impressed with Floral Design 39

Cizao Kiln Green Glazed Dish Impressed with Floral Design 40

Cizao Kiln Brown Glazed Jar 41

Cizao Kiln Brown Glazed Jar with Four Rings 42

Dehua Kiln Blue and White Glazed Jar with Double Rings Impressed with Floral Design 43

Dehua Kiln Blue and White Glazed Gourd Vase 44

Dehua Kiln Blue and White Glazed Vase with Horn-shaped Rim Impressed with Floral Design 45

Dehua Kiln Blue and White Glazed Cosmetic Box …………………………………………… 46

Bronze Ring…………………………………………………………………………………………………47

Southern Song Dynasty Shipwreck "Banyangjiao I" ……………………………… 48

Fuqing Dongzhang Kiln Small Cup with Hare's Fur Glaze ………………………………… 50

Fuqing Dongzhang Kiln Black Glazed Small Cup ……………………………………………… 52

Fujian Blue and White Glazed Bowl with Unglazed Rim and Flowers Design …………………… 54

Fujian Blue and White Glazed Bowl with Unglazed Rim and Flowers and Fishes Design …… 55

Fujian Blue and White Glazed Bowl with Unglazed Rim and Children Playing Design ………… 56

Fuqing Dongzhang Kiln Brown Glazed Basin with Leaves Design……………………………… 57

Yuan Dynasty Suizhong Sandaogang Shipwreck ……………………………… 58

Cizhou Kiln White Glazed Basin with a Fish in a Pond in Brown Pigment …………………… 60

Cizhou Kiln White Glazed Jar with Floral Design in Brown Pigment ……………………………61

Cizhou Kiln White Glazed Jar with Dragon and Phoenix Design in Brown Pigment …………… 62

Cizhou Kiln Black and White Glazed Bowl with Leaves Design …………………………………… 64

Cizhou Kiln Black and White Glazed Bowl with Leaves Design …………………………………… 65

Cizhou Kiln Black and White Glazed Bowl……………………………………………………………… 66

Cizhou Kiln Black Glazed Bowl with Chrysanthemum Petals ……………………………………… 67

Cizhou Kiln Black Glazed Bowl with Chrysanthemum Petals ……………………………………… 68

Cizhou Kiln White Glazed Lid with Leaves Design in Brown Pigment ………………………… 70

Cizhou Kiln White Glazed Lid with Spiral Design in Brown Pigment ………………………… 71

Cizhou Kiln White Glazed Dish with Leaves Design in Brown Pigment……………………… 72

Cizhou Kiln White Glazed Dish with Leaves Design in Brown Pigment……………………… 73

Cizhou Kiln White Glazed Dish with Leaves Design in Brown Pigment………………………74

Cizhou Kiln White Glazed Dish with Leaves Design in Brown Pigment……………………… 75

Cizhou Kiln White Glazed Vase …………………………………………………………………………76

Ming Dynasty Shipwreck "Nan'ao I" ……………………………………………… 78

Jingdezhen Kiln Blue-and-white Bowl with String Pattern ………………………………… 80

Jingdezhen Kiln Blue-and-white Bowl with String Pattern	81
Jingdezhen Kiln Blue-and-white Bowl with Fish, Dragon and Waves	82
Jingdezhen Kiln Blue-and-white Bowl with Fish, Dragon and Waves	83
Jingdezhen Kiln Blue-and-white Large Bowl with Conch and Dragon	84
Jingdezhen Kiln Blue-and-white Large Bowl with Flower Scrolls and Grapevines	85
Jingdezhen Kiln Blue-and-white Cup with a Figure and *Fu* Inscription	86
Jingdezhen Kiln Blue-and-white Cup with a Figure and *Fu* Inscription	87
Jingdezhen Kiln Blue-and-white Cup with Flowers and Birds	88
Jingdezhen Kiln Blue-and-white Cup with Orchids Sprays	89
Jingdezhen Kiln Blue-and-white Cup with Peony Scrolls and *Fu* Inscription	90
Jingdezhen Kiln Blue-and-white Cup with Flower Sprays and *Fu* Inscription	91
Jingdezhen Kiln Blue-and-white Plate with Phoenix Towards the Sun	92
Jingdezhen Kiln Blue-and-white Plate with Trees, Stone and Railing	93
Jingdezhen Kiln Blue-and-white Plate with Trees, Stone and Railing	94
Zhangzhou Kiln Blue-and-white Plate with Chrysanthemum Design	95
Zhangzhou Kiln Blue-and-white Plate with Qilin Design and Flat Rim	96
Zhangzhou Kiln Blue-and-white Bottle with Flower Scrolls	97
Zhangzhou Kiln Blue-and-white Dish with Chrysanthemum Design	98
Zhangzhou Kiln Blue-and-white Dish with Chrysanthemum Design	99
Zhangzhou Kiln Blue-and-white Small Jar with Flower Scrolls	100
Zhangzhou Kiln Blue-and-white Small Jar with Flower Scrolls	101
Zhangzhou Kiln Blue-and-white Bottle with Flower Scrolls	102
Jingdezhen Kiln Famille Verte Cosmetic Box with Rabbit and Flower Sprays	104

Qing Dynasty Shipwreck "Wanjiao I" 106

Jingdezhen Kiln Blue-and-white Bowl with Children Playing Design	108
Jingdezhen Kiln Blue-and-white Bowl with Landscape Scene	109
Jingdezhen Kiln Blue-and-white Bowl with Landscape Scene	110
Jingdezhen Kiln Blue-and-white Bowl with Flowers Design	111

Jingdezhen Kiln Blue-and-white Plate with Flower Sprays 112

Jingdezhen Kiln Blue-and-white Dish with Phoenix amid Peony Scrolls 113

Jingdezhen Kiln Blue-and-white Plate with Chrysanthemum Posies 114

Jingdezhen Kiln Blue-and-white Lobed Plate with Chrysanthemum Posies 116

Jingdezhen Kiln Blue-and-white Lobed Plate with Stones and Flower Sprays 118

Jingdezhen Kiln Plate with Plum Blossom Reserved in White on Blue Ground 120

Jingdezhen Kiln Blue-and-white Plate with Plum and Bamboos Design Decorated in Underglazed Blue and Red 122

Jingdezhen Kiln Blue-and-white Stem Cup 124

Jingdezhen Kiln Blue-and-white Cup with Chrysanthemum Sprays 125

Jingdezhen Kiln Famille Verte Plate with Auspicious Treasures 126

Jingdezhen Kiln Famille Verte Plate with Flower Sprays and Vases 128

Qing Dynasty Shipwreck "Xiaobaijiao I" 130

Jingdezhen Kiln Blue-and-white Bowl with Dated Inscription of Jiaqing Reign and Flower Scrolls 132

Jingdezhen Kiln Blue-and-white Bowl with Dated Inscription of Daoguang Reign and Flower Scrolls 134

Jingdezhen Kiln Blue-and-white Bowl with Flower Scrolls 135

Jingdezhen Kiln Blue-and-white Lobed Stem Plate with Floral Design 136

Jingdezhen Kiln Blue-and-white Lobed Stem Plate with Floral Design 138

Jingdezhen Kiln Blue-and-white Plate with Fungus Design 140

Jingdezhen Kiln Blue-and-white Plate with Chrysanthemum Petals and *Fu* Inscription 142

Jingdezhen Kiln Blue-and-white Dish with Flowers Design 143

Jingdezhen Kiln Blue-and-white Lamp with Floral Scrolls 144

Jingdezhen Kiln Blue-and-white Cup with Flowers Design 146

Jingdezhen Kiln Blue-and-white Spoon with Floral Design 147

Jingdezhen Kiln Famille Verte Jar 148

Yixing Clay Teapot 150

Yixing Clay Jar 151

Brown Glazed Ewer 152

Seal with *Yuanheshengji* Inscription 153

Spanish Silver Coin 154

Sounding Lead 155

Zhongshan Warship 156

Wooden Badge with Inscription *Zhongshan* 158

Mauser Pistol 159

79 Rifle 160

79 Rifle Bayonet 161

Wrench 162

Artillery Shell 163

Brush Pot Made of Artillery Shell 164

Inkstone 165

Letter Opener 166

Telegram Manuscript 167

Copper Button 168

Shaver 169

Canteen 170

Soda Pop Bottle with Inscription *Hankouzanyu* 171

Two-handle Enamel Mug with Inscription *Jicang* 172

Enamel Washbasin with Inscription *Pinghai* 173

Torch 174

Wall Mount Clothes Hanger 175

Portable Lamp 176

Postscript 178

概述 Introduction

水下考古的出现，距今不过100多年。19世纪中叶，瑞士湖上居址的确认与调查、发掘，标志着水下考古学的萌芽；20世纪初期，头带硬盔的原始管供重潜技术发明并在沉船打捞上得到了初步运用；1943年，法国海军发明自携式水下呼吸器（轻潜技术）后，人类在水下才有了较多的呼吸自由，考古学家较长时间潜入水下进行调查和发掘作业的梦想开始得以实现；20世纪40至50年代，法、英、美等国考古学者开始采用轻潜技术，对地中海的水下历史遗存进行了调查与发掘；1960年，美国考古学家乔治·巴斯（George Bass）应邀对土耳其格里多亚角（Cape Gelidonya）海域公元7世纪拜占庭时期的沉船遗址进行调查和发掘时，开创性地在水下实践了考古学方法，成为水下考古发展史上的一个里程碑式事件；随后，一些国家与地区在各地海域也逐渐开展了水下考古工作，不断完善和发展了水下考古技术与方法，并逐步确立了水下考古学这一独特的学科体系。

水下考古进入中国，迄今不过20多年。1986年，英国人米歇尔·哈彻（Michel Harcher）在中国南海盗掘大批中国清代康熙年间的青花瓷器等珍贵文物后，在荷兰首都阿姆斯特丹大肆拍卖，引发了考古学界、博物馆学界和社会各界的强烈不满，并引起了中国政府及文物部门的高度关注。1987年，国家文物局牵头成立了"国家水下考古协调小组"，随后在原中国历史博物馆（现中国国家博物馆）建立了我国第一个水下考古专业机构。嗣后20多年间，国家和地方不断强化投入与支持力度，极大推动了我国水下考古在机构布局、人才培养、技术装备、项目开展、科技保护、合作交流以及法规体系与学科建设诸方面的长足发展。特别是2009年12月国家水下文化遗产保护中心挂牌组建、2014年7月国家文物局水下文化遗产保护中心正式成立后，我国的水下考古工作逐步向全方位的水下文化遗产保护方向发展，工作领域亦逐步从近海海域扩展到远海海域和内陆水域，"国家主导，部门协作，地方参与"的水下文化遗产保护格局开始逐步形成。

2014年10月，首个全面、系统反映我国水下考古20多年发展历程和主要成就的

专题性水下考古陈列——"水下考古在中国"专题陈列在刚刚落成的国家水下文化遗产保护宁波基地正式对外开放。在陈列内容上,"水下考古在中国"专题陈列从"机构与队伍"、"技术与方法"、"调查与发掘"、"保护与交流"、"规划与展望"五个层面着手铺展,既反映我国水下考古发展历程中的重大事件,也兼顾为之作出重要贡献的人物,力争做到见人见事;既具有水下考古学科的专业性,也不乏面向广大公众的普及性,力争做到雅俗共赏;既汇总各地水下考古以往的重点项目与主要成就,也突出体现宁波水下考古特别是象山渔山"小白礁Ⅰ号"水下考古的重要成果,力争做到点面结合。在陈列形式上,"水下考古在中国"专题陈列利用展厅独特的建筑格局创造出全开放和半开放有机结合的空间环境与参观路线,主要采取出水文物与技术装备展品、模拟复原与真实工作场景相结合,以及多媒体互动、电子幕墙等其他各类现代辅助展陈的手段,寓乐于教,寓教于乐,为人们讲述我国水下考古最真实也最生动的故事。

"水下考古在中国"专题陈列开放尚不满一年时间,已经吸引了超过40万人次前往参观游览。考虑到陈列所在的国家水下文化遗产保护宁波基地远在位于东海之滨的北仑春晓滨海新城,即使距离宁波市区也有百里之遥,这一参观人数无疑显得尤为难得。也因为这样,正式出版这样的一本图录,以便更好、更广地宣传展示我国水下考古的主要成果,并借此简要回顾陈列推出的前后过程,感谢为陈列作出贡献的各个单位和各界人士,既是必要的,也是值得的。

"水下考古在中国"专题陈列之所以选择落户于宁波基地,我们认为主要是基于以下三个方面的考量:

其一,是对宁波水下考古工作的认可。众所周知,地处我国大陆海岸线中段、长江三角洲东南翼的宁波,自古以来就是我国重要的对外交通贸易口岸,是中国大运河最南端的出海口和"海上丝绸之路"的始发港之一,发展水下考古具有得天独厚的地缘优势、丰富的资源优势和敢为人前的先发优势:

在机构建设上,1998年12月9日,我国首个水下考古工作站——原中国历史博物馆水下考古宁波工作站(2008年升格为中国国家博物馆水下考古宁波基地)已选择在宁波市文物考古研究所内挂牌成立,从此拉开了宁波发展水下考古事业的历史序幕;2010年7月29日,国家文物局水下文化遗产保护中心组建后的首个国家水下文化遗产保护基地——国家水下文化遗产保护宁波基地又在宁波北仑春晓滨海新城挂牌奠基,由此揭开了宁波水下考古走向水下文化遗产保护的崭新篇章;2012年5月11

日，国家水下文化遗产保护宁波基地象山工作站揭牌，它是我国第一个县级水下文化遗产保护工作站。

在人才建设上，宁波派员参加了几乎所有的全国性水下考古培训和国家组织的国内外重大水下考古活动，并先后承办了第二期"全国水下考古专业人员培训班"（1998年）和首届"国家水下文化遗产保护（考古）培训班"（2011年）。目前，宁波共拥有水下考古队员10名，其中仍坚持在一线作业的水下考古队员达8名之多，专业人才数量稳居全国前列，被誉为"水下考古的宁波帮"，已然成为我国水下文化遗产保护的一支重要力量。

在业务建设上，宁波在全国率先提出将水下文物调查纳入"三普"范畴并付诸实践，也率先制定了水下文物普查的技术规范并在全国各地推广；2012至2014年间，由国家文物局水下文化遗产保护中心与宁波市文物考古研究所（国家水下文化遗产保护宁波基地）共同组织实施的"小白礁Ⅰ号"水下考古发掘项目，因其先进的工作理念、科学的考古方法、创新的科技应用、超前的保护意识和多重的安全保障等为业界和社会所称道，被誉为"我国水下考古走向水下文化遗产保护的又一重要标识"、"我国水下考古的又一创新之作"。有鉴于此，国家经考虑，最终同意"水下考古在中国"专题陈列落户宁波基地，成为与"水下考古·宁波论坛"瑜亮并辉的两大国家级水下考古品牌。

其二，是对国家水下文化遗产保护宁波基地的支持。2010年7月29日，我国首个国家水下文化遗产保护基地——宁波基地暨宁波中国港口博物馆建设工程在美丽的北仑春晓滨海新城隆重奠基，工程总占地面积约51966平方米，总建筑面积约40987平方米，总投资约7.3亿元，由北仑区人民政府全额投资建设。其中，宁波基地建筑面积约11000平方米，主要设有陈列展示区、保护修复区、收藏整理区、培训交流区、研究办公区、文体活动区、公寓宿舍区等不同功能区块，并将逐步打造成为我国水下考古的重要工作平台和学术交流的重要科研阵地。

宁波基地建设伊始，我们即提出了举办"水下考古在中国"专题陈列的初步构想，得到了国家有关方面的首肯，并委托我们全权负责陈列大纲的编制工作。2012年9月11日，我们在北仑体育宾馆召开了"水下考古在中国"专题陈列论证会，时任中国文化遗产研究院院长兼国家水下文化遗产保护中心主任的刘曙光、时任国家水下文化遗产保护中心副主任的范伊然、时任中国国家博物馆水下考古研究中心主任的赵嘉斌、中国国家博物馆美术工作部副主任翟睿、中国国家博物馆设计室副主任李京擘、广东省博物馆馆长魏峻、福建博物院研究员栗建安、时任浙江省文物局文物保护与考古处副调研员的许常丰、宁波市文化广电新闻出版局副局长孟建耀、北仑区文化广电新闻出版局副局长乐静毅、北仑博物馆馆长冯毅，以及编制单位代表对陈列大纲进行了认真论证，发表了中肯意见。会后，我们根据论证意见对陈列大纲作了较大幅度的调整，并再次征求各方意见，获得一致通过后，始交付展陈设计单位——北京天图设计工程有限公司设计布展。

2014年10月16日，历经四年艰苦建设并在全国率先建成的宁波基地正式竣工投用，设于宁波基地水下考古专题陈列室与出水沉船修复展示室内、展陈面积达2000平方米的"水下考古在中国"专题陈列同步对外开放，一举成为宁波基地落成盛典的重头戏和为广大市民奉献上的一道文化盛宴。

其三，也是最重要的，"水下考古在中国"专题陈列落户宁波基地并按期顺利开放，是国家、省、市、区上下联动和社会各界通力协作的成果。值此宁波基地落成投用、专题陈列对外开放周年将届之际，我们谨向以下单位和个人表示诚挚的感谢：

致谢单位

国家文物局
国家文物局水下文化遗产保护中心
中国文化遗产研究院
中国国家博物馆
辽宁省文物考古研究所
葫芦岛市文化广播影视局
葫芦岛市博物馆
湖北省文物局
武汉中山舰博物馆
福州市文物局
福州市文物考古工作队
龙海市文化广电体育局
龙海市博物馆
广东省文物局
广东海上丝绸之路博物馆
浙江省文物局

宁波市文化广电新闻出版局
北仑区委、区政府
北仑区委宣传部
北仑区文化广电新闻出版局
北仑区建筑工务局
宁波中国港口博物馆（北仑博物馆）
宁波建工集团
北京天图设计工程有限公司
……

致谢个人

文化部副部长、国家文物局局长	励小捷
文化部党组成员、故宫博物院院长	单霁翔
国家文物局副局长	童明康
国家文物局副局长	顾玉才
国家文物局副局长	宋新潮
国家文物局文物保护与考古司司长	关　强
国家文物局办公室副主任	闫亚林
国家文物局文物保护与考古司考古处处长	张　磊
国家文物局政策法规司新闻与宣传处处长	范伊然
国家文物局文物保护与考古司文物处副处长	张　凌
中国文化遗产研究院院长	刘曙光
国家文物局水下文化遗产保护中心主任	柴晓明
国家文物局水下文化遗产保护中心党支部书记	张　威
国家文物局水下文化遗产保护中心水下考古所所长	姜　波
国家文物局水下文化遗产保护中心办公室主任	赵嘉斌
国家文物局水下文化遗产保护中心技术与装备处副主任	李　滨
国家文物局水下文化遗产保护中心	邓启江
国家文物局水下文化遗产保护中心	孟原召
国家文物局水下文化遗产保护中心	梁国庆
中国国家博物馆美术工作部副主任	翟　睿

中国国家博物馆设计室副主任	李京璧
辽宁省文物考古研究所所长	吴炎亮
辽宁省文物考古研究所原副所长	华玉冰
葫芦岛市博物馆馆长	孙建军
湖北省文物局副局长	王风竹
武汉中山舰博物馆馆长	王瑞华
福建博物院研究员	栗建安
福建博物院文物考古研究所副所长	羊泽林
福州市文物考古工作队队长	林 果
龙海市博物馆馆长	郑 云
广东省博物馆馆长	魏 峻
广东海上丝绸之路博物馆馆长	黄铁坚
浙江省文化厅原巡视员、省文物局原局长	鲍贤伦
浙江省文化厅副厅长、省文物局局长	陈 瑶
浙江省文化厅副巡视员、省文物局副局长	吴志强
浙江省文物局副局长	郑建华
浙江省文物局文物保护与考古处副处长	许常丰
宁波市委原常委、北仑区委原书记	陈利幸
宁波市委常委、北仑区委书记	马卫光
宁波市文化广电新闻出版局原局长	陈佳强
宁波市文化广电新闻出版局局长	赵惠峰
宁波市文化广电新闻出版局副局长	孟建耀
宁波市文化广电新闻出版局副局长	舒月明
宁波市文化广电新闻出版局文物与博物馆处处长	徐建成
北仑区人民政府原区长	华 伟
北仑区人民政府区长	胡 奎
北仑区委常委、宣传部原部长	叶 苗
北仑区委常委、宣传部部长	杨 劲
北仑区人民政府原副区长	丁素贞
北仑区人民政府副区长	陆亚芬
北仑区政协副主席	袁 侠
北仑区委宣传部副部长	楼宏斌

北仑区文化广电新闻出版局局长	陈胜蛟
北仑区文化广电新闻出版局副局长	乐静毅
北仑区文化广电新闻出版局副局长	凌晓军
宁波中国港口博物馆（北仑博物馆）馆长	冯　毅
宁波中国港口博物馆（北仑博物馆）副馆长	王昌海
宁波中国港口博物馆（北仑博物馆）副馆长	陈卫立

……

最后，我们要说的是，我国水下考古虽然只走过了短短20多年的历程，却取得了举世瞩目的辉煌成就。而作为首个全面、系统反映我国水下考古20多年发展历程与主要成就的"水下考古在中国"专题陈列，虽然由于种种原因，一些重要的水下考古出水文物未能在陈列中展出，现有陈列的内容与表现形式也仍有进一步改进提升的空间，但它毕竟用形象、生动、真实、多彩的现代展陈语言，将一颗颗耀眼的珍珠缀连起来，构成我国古代海洋文明的长链，既可让我们牢记曾经走过的道路，也让我们对于明天充满美好的憧憬。同时，我们也有理由相信，这本浓缩了陈列菁华的图录的正式付梓出版，必将使我国水下考古的种子在更加广阔的空间传播，并在未来结出更加丰硕的果实。

主要参考资料

1. 宁波市文物考古研究所、国家水下文化遗产保护宁波基地：《"水下考古在中国"专题陈列大纲》，2014，内部资料。

2. 宁波市文物考古研究所、国家水下文化遗产保护宁波基地，王结华执笔：《风雨兼程十六载——宁波水下考古的回顾与展望》，载《中国文物报》2014年9月26日第5版。

3. 王结华：《十年磨一剑，今朝破水出——"小白礁Ⅰ号"折射下的宁波水下考古》，载国家文物局水下文化遗产保护中心、宁波市文物考古研究所：《水下24米——浙江宁波象山"小白礁Ⅰ号"水下考古实录》，第150-162页，中国广播电视出版社，2014年6月第1版。

4. 宁波市文物考古研究所、国家文物局水下文化遗产保护中心，林国聪、王结华、姜波执笔：《我国水下考古的又一创新之作——浙江宁波象山"小白礁Ⅰ号"2014年度发掘》，载《中国文物报》2014年8月29日第5版。

5. 宁波中国港口博物馆、国家水下文化遗产保护宁波基地、宁波市文物考古研究所，楼宏斌、王结华、冯毅执笔：《众志成城铸华章——宁波中国港口博物馆与国家水下文化遗产保护宁波基地建设巡礼》，载《中国文物报》2014年10月10日第6-7版。

Introduction

The history of underwater archaeology is about a hundred years. The emergence of the subject appeared in the mid-19th century when the prehistoric pile dwelling site in Lake Zurich had been identified, surveyed and excavated using archaeological methods. In the early 20th century, the invention of Surface-supplied diving dress had been applied to the shipwreck salvage activity. The goal of staying underwater for a relatively long time was reached in 1943 when the French navy invented the technique of open-circuit Self-Contained Underwater Breathing Apparatus (SCUBA) which provided the diver with a substantial amount of available air in the water. From 1940s to 1950s, the underwater archaeologists from France, America and Britain started to explore the underwater cultural and historical heritage in Mediterranean using the SCUBA diving technique. In addition, the American underwater archaeologist George Bass adopted the archaeological methods into the shipwreck excavation when he was invited to survey and excavate the 7th century Byzantine shipwreck site in Cape Gelidonya, which has been valued as a milestone in the development of underwater archaeology. Later the underwater archaeological surveys and excavations have been conducted in a series of countries and areas. The underwater archaeology has instituted its technique and methodology and has gradually developed into a unique academic discipline.

The history of underwater archaeology in China is only more than two decades. In 1986, Englishman Michel Harcher salvaged and smuggled a great number of blue-and-white wares dated in Kangxi Reign of Qing Dynasty from South China Sea and sold the artefacts in Amsterdam auction. The crime has not only generated the discontent in the fields of Archaeology, Museology and general public, but also highly attracted the attention from the Chinese Central Government and the Chinese Cultural Heritage Department. In 1987, the National Underwater Archaeological Group was established after its proposal by the State Administration of Cultural Heritage. Based on this group, the Chinese Underwater Archaeological Institute was established at the Chinese Historical Museum (now the National Museum of China). Over the following 20 years, the central and local governments have strongly supported the underwater archaeological institutes in the aspects of establishment, staff training, equipment improvement, project undertaking, scientific conservation, academic communication, legislative regulation and subject construction. Especially after the establishment of the National Center of Underwater Cultural Heritage in December, 2009 and the establishment of the Underwater Cultural Heritage Center of the State Administration of Cultural Heritage in July, 2014, Chinese underwater archaeology changed its focus to protect China's underwater relics and heritage. Fieldwork extended from the coastal areas to deep seas and inland waters. The study principle of "leading by government, supporting by institute, and participating with local authorities" was proposed to start protecting China's underwater heritage.

In October, 2014, the exhibition *Underwater Archaeology in China* located in Ningbo Base, National Center of Underwater Cultural Heritage was opened to the public. The exhibition is the first special-subject display in underwater archaeology which has comprehensively and systematically introduced the development and achievements of Chinese Underwater Archaeology over the last two decades. The content has been divided into five sections, as "Institutes and Staff", "Techniques and Methodologies", "Surveys and Excavations", "Preservation and Communication" and "Plans and Expectations", aiming to not only reflect the major events in the development of Chinese Underwater Archaeology, but also present the important figures who had involved in the events; not only summarize the key projects and the significant achievements across the country, but also emphasize the underwater archaeological achievements in Ningbo, especially the major accomplishments such as the project of "Xiaobaijiao Ⅰ" shipwreck. The exhibition has also utilized its unique construction design to create a visiting route that integrates both fully open and semi-open spaces. In addition, not only are the multiple display objects presented in the exhibition, including the traditional artefacts, the diving equipment, the site replicas and working process replicas, but also multiple display methods are adopted including multimedia interaction, electronic curtain wall, etc., It is designed to tell the stories of Chinese underwater archaeology and to educate the public in an entertaining way.

The exhibition of *Underwater Archaeology in China* has only opened to the public for less than a year, but with the visitors over 0.4 million. Considered the far location of the exhibition and the Ningbo Base, which is in Chunxiao Town of Beilun District, about a hundred miles away from the Ningbo urban area, the 0.4 million visitor number becomes a sound evidence of the popularity of the display. Therefore, in order to appreciate the support of the audience, here we officially publish the atlas of the display and review the establishment of the exhibition in this article to widespread the achievements of the Chinese underwater archaeology to the public, as well as to thank the staff who had made their contributions to the exhibition.

The exhibition of *Underwater Archaeology in China* has chosen its location in Ningbo Base for three following reasons:

First of all, it is the acknowledgment of Ningbo underwater archaeology. Located in the middle of the mainland coastal line and southeast of Yangtze River Delta, Ningbo City has been known as an important port for foreign communication and trade since the ancient time. It was once the southernmost estuary of China Grand Canal and one of the original ports of the "Maritime Silk Road". With the great advantages in geographic, academic, historical and talent resources, Ningbo has developed its underwater archaeology one step ahead.

The first underwater archaeology station as Ningbo Underwater Archaeology Station of Chinese Historical Museum was established in 9th of December, 1998 (The institute was upgraded as Ningbo Underwater Archaeology Base of National Museum of China in 2008), which marked the beginning of the underwater archaeology in Ningbo. In 29th of July, 2010, proposed by the National Center of Underwater Cultural Heritage, the first national underwater cultural heritage base was established in Chunxiao Town of Beilun District of Ningbo as Ningbo Base, National Center of Underwater Cultural Heritage. The establishment of the Ningbo Base is a milestone in the development of Ningbo underwater archaeology. In addition, the Base set its first working station in Xiangshan County of Ningbo in 11th of May, 2012, which became the first underwater cultural heritage working station in county level in the national scale.

Ningbo has always focused on the talents development and has its underwater archaeologists participated in almost all the national underwater archaeological trainings and foreign underwater archaeological projects organized by the Chinese government. Moreover, Ningbo has held "The Second National Underwater Archaeologist Training Session" in 1998 and "The First National Underwater Cultural Heritage Conservation (Archaeology) Session" in 2011. Now the Ningbo Base owns 10 underwater archaeologists, among whom 8 are still participating underwater projects every year. The quantity and the quality of the experts in the Base are outstanding even on the national level and have been highly praised as "the Ningbo Group in Chinese Underwater Archaeology". Besides, the experts in Ningbo have also become an important force in China's underwater cultural heritage conservation.

Ningbo was the first to propose that the underwater cultural heritage should be concluded in the scale of the Third National Cultural Heritage General Investigation and the first to conduct the proposal. Ningbo was also the first to institute the regulation for underwater investigation of underwater cultural heri-tage and archaeological sites. The regulation has then been promoted across the country. Moreover, from 2012 to 2014, the National Center of Underwater Cultural Heritage and Ningbo Municipal Institute of Cultural Relics and Archaeology (Ningbo Base, National Center of Underwater Cultural Heritage) cooperated to accomplish the excavation of "Xiaobaijiao I" shipwreck. The underwater excavation project was highly valued for its advanced working concepts, scientific archaeological methods, innovative scientific application, anticipatory protection awareness and multiple security progress, and was considered as "another important mark in the development of China from underwater archaeology to underwater cultural heritage protection" and "another innovative work in Chinese underwater archaeology". Therefore, with all the achievements, the government had finally authorized the establishment of *Underwater Archaeology in China* exhibition in Ningbo Base, and the exhibition becomes another important brand for the Base other than the Ningbo Conference of Underwater Archaeology.

The second reason is the great support that the Central Government of China has given to the Ningbo Base, National Center of Underwater Cultural Heritage. In 29th of July, 2010, the construction of the first national underwater cultural heritage base, Ningbo Base was started in Chunxiao Town of Beilun District of Ningbo. The whole construction covers an area of 51,966 square meters, and the building takes 40,987 square meters. The construction was fully funded by the Beilun District Government with the funds of 730 million *yuan*(RMB). Ningbo Base takes 11,000 square meters in the construction, with different function areas such as Display Area, Conservation Area, Collection Area, Training Area, Office, Gym and Accommodation. The final goal of the Base is to become a key working platform of Chinese underwater archaeology and a research center for academic communication.

From the beginning of the construction, the proposal of holding the exhibition *Underwater Archaeology in China* was raised and approved by the relevant governmental departments. Our first mission was to edit the outline of the display. In 11th of September, 2012, the symposium of *Underwater Archaeology in China* Exhibition was held in Beilun Gym Hotel. Then Head of Chinese Academy of Cultural Heritage and Then Director of National Center of Underwater Cultural Heritage Liu Shuguang, Then Deputy Director of National Center of Underwater Cultural Heritage Fan Yiran, Then Director of Underwater Archaeology Research Centre of National Museum of China Zhao Jiabin, Deputy Director of Art Work Department of National Museum of China Zhai Rui, Deputy Director of Designing Department of National Museum of China Li Jingbo, Curator of Guangdong Museum Wei Jun, Researcher of Fujian Museum Li Jian'an, Then Associate Consultant of Cultural Relics Conservation and Archaeology Department of Zhejiang Provincial Administration of Cultural Heritage Xu Changfeng, Deputy General Director of Culture, Radio, Television, Press and Publication Bureau of Ningbo Meng Jianyao, Deputy General Director of Culture, Radio, Television, Press and Publication Bureau of Beilun District Le Jingyi, Curator of Beilun Museum Feng Yi and members from related institutes participated the symposium. The experts discussed the outline in the symposium and offered pertinent opinions, based on which the outline was substantially modified afterwards. The second version of the outline was highly affirmed and received an unanimous approval when we solicited the opinions from the public. It was then the final outline was given to the exhibition company Tiantu Cultural & Creative Industry

Group to design the exhibition.

After four-year construction, on 16th of October, 2014, Ningbo Base became the first underwater cultural heritage base that came into service, within which the *Underwater Archaeology in China* exhibition occupies the Display Area and Conservation Area of the Base, with a total space of 2,000 square meters. The exhibition was opened to the public at the same time when the Base came into service, together providing a cultural feast to the local citizens of Ningbo.

The last but not the least, the successful establishment of *Underwater Archaeology in China* exhibition owes to the support from the society and the cooperation and efforts of the associated institutes. Here at the anniversary of the establishment of the exhibition and the completion of the Ningbo Base, we would like to send our gratitude to:

State Administration of Cultural Heritage
National Center of Underwater Cultural Heritage
Chinese Academy of Cultural Heritage
National Museum of China
Liaoning Provincial Cultural Relics and Archaeological Research Institute
Huludao Municipal Cultural, Radio and Television Bureau
Huludao Museum
Hubei Provincial Administration of Cultural Heritage
Wuhan Zhongshan Warship Museum
Fuzhou Municipal Administration of Cultural Heritage
Fuzhou Municipal Institute of Cultural Relics and Archaeology
Longhai Municipal Culture, Radio, Television and Sport Bureau
Longhai Museum
Guangdong Provincial Administration of Cultural Heritage
Maritime Silk Road Museum of Guangdong
Zhejiang Provincial Administration of Cultural Heritage
Ningbo Municipal Culture, Radio, Television, Press and Publication Bureau
Beilun District Committee, Beilun District Government
Beilun District Publicity Department
Culture, Radio, Television, Press and Publication Bureau of Beilun District
Construction Works Bureau of Beilun District
China Port Museum (Beilun Museum)
Ningbo Construction Co.,Ltd

Tiantu Cultural&Creative Industry Group
……
We would like to express our gratitude to:

Deputy Minister of Ministry of Culture, General Director of State Administration of Cultural Heritage	Li Xiaojie
Party Member of Ministry of Culture, Curator of Palace Museum	Shan Jixiang
Deputy General Director of State Administration of Cultural Heritage	Tong Mingkang
Deputy General Director of State Administration of Cultural Heritage	Gu Yucai
Deputy General Director of State Administration of Cultural Heritage	Song Xinchao
Director General of Cultural Relics Conservation and Archaeology Department of State Administration of Cultural Heritage	Guan Qiang
Deputy Director of Office of State Administration of Cultural Heritage	Yan Yalin
Director of Archaeology Division of Cultural Relics Conservation and Archaeology Department of State Administration of Cultural Heritage	Zhang Lei
Director of News and Propaganda Division of Policies and Laws Department of State Administration of Cultural Heritage	Fan Yiran
Deputy Director of Cultural Relics Division of Cultural Relics Conservation and Archaeology Department of State Administration of Cultural Heritage	Zhang Ling
Head of Chinese Academy of Cultural Heritage	Liu Shuguang
Director of National Center of Underwater Cultural Heritage	Chai Xiaoming
Party Branch Secretary of National Center of Underwater Cultural Heritage	Zhang Wei
Director of Underwater Archaeology Department of National Center of Underwater Cultural Heritage	Jiang Bo
Director of the office of National Center of Underwater Cultural Heritage	Zhao Jiabin
Deputy Director of Technical and Equipment Department of National Center of Underwater Cultural Heritage	Li Bin
National Center of Underwater Cultural Heritage	Deng Qijiang
National Center of Underwater Cultural Heritage	Meng Yuanzhao

National Center of Underwater Cultural Heritage	Liang Guoqing
Deputy Director of Art Work Department of National Museum of China	Zhai Rui
Deputy Director of Designing Department of National Museum of China	Li Jingbo
Director of Liaoning Provincial Cultural Relics and Archaeological Research Institute	Wu Yanliang
Former Deputy Director of Liaoning Provincial Cultural Relics and Archaeological Research Institute	Hua Yubing
Curator of Huludao Museum	Sun Jianjun
Deputy General Director of Hubei Provincial Administration of Cultural Heritage	Wang Fengzhu
Curator of Wuhan Zhongshan Warship Museum	Wang Ruihua
Researcher of Fujian Museum	Li Jian'an
Deputy Director of Cultural Relics and Archaeology Institute of Fujian Musuem	Yang Zelin
Director of Fuzhou Municipal Institute of Cultural Relics and Archaeology	Lin Guo
Curator of Longhai Museum	Zheng Yun
Curator of Guangdong Museum	Wei Jun
Curator of Maritime Silk Road Museum of Guangdong	Huang Tiejian
Former Inspector of Cultural Department of Zhejiang Province, Former Director of Zhejiang Provincial Administration of Cultural Heritage	Bao Xianlun
Deputy Director of Cultural Department of Zhejiang Province, Director of Zhejiang Provincial Administration of Cultural Heritage	Chen Yao
Deputy Inspector of Cultural Department of Zhejiang Province, Deputy Director of Zhejiang Provincial Administration of Cultural Heritage	Wu Zhiqiang
Deputy Director General of Zhejiang Provincial Administration of Cultural Heritage	Zheng Jianhua
Deputy Director of Cultural Relics Conservation and Archaeology Department of Zhejiang Provincial Administration of Cultural Heritage	Xu Changfeng
Former Member of the Ningbo Municipal Standing Committee, Former Beilun District Secretary of the Party Committee	Chen Lixing
Member of the Ningbo Municipal Standing Committee, Beilun District Secretary of the Party Committee	Ma Weiguang

Former General Director of Culture, Radio, Television, Press and Publication Bureau of Ningbo	Chen Jiaqiang
General Director of Culture, Radio, Television, Press and Publication Bureau of Ningbo	Zhao Huifeng
Deputy General Director of Culture, Radio, Television, Press and Publication Bureau of Ningbo	Meng Jianyao
Deputy General Director of Culture, Radio, Television, Press and Publication Bureau of Ningbo	Shu Yueming
Director of Cultural Relics and Museum Department of Culture, Radio, Television, Press and Publication Bureau of Ningbo	Xu Jiancheng
Former Mayor of Beilun District Government	Hua Wei
Mayor of Beilun District Government	Hu Kui
Member of the Beilun District Standing Committee, Former Director of Beilun District Publicity Department	Ye Miao
Member of the Beilun District Standing Committee, Director of Beilun District Publicity Department	Yang Jing
Former Deputy Mayor of Beilun District Government	Ding Suzhen
Deputy District Mayor of Beilun District Government	Lu Yafen
Deputy Chairman of Beilun District CPPCC	Yuan Xia
Deputy Director of Beilun District Propaganda Department	Lou Hongbin
General Director of Culture, Radio, Television, Press and Publication Bureau of Beilun District	Chen Shengjiao
Deputy General Director of Culture, Radio, Television, Press and Publication Bureau of Beilun District	Le Jingyi
Deputy General Director of Culture, Radio, Television, Press and Publication Bureau of Beilun District	Ling Xiaojun
Curator of China Port Museum (Beilun Museum)	Feng Yi
Deputy Curator of China Port Museum (Beilun Museum)	Wang Changhai
Deputy Curator of China Port Museum (Beilun Museum)	Chen Weili

……

Finally, although the history of Chinese underwater archaeology is only more than 20 years, the achievements it gains has already drawn the attention from all over the world. As the first comprehensive and systematical reflection of China's underwater archaeology history, *Underwater Archaeology in China* exhibition uses iconic, vivid, authentic and colorful display language to present the glorious ancient marine civilization. It reminds us of the precious past, and also depicts the bright future. We have the confidence that the publication of this book would spread the knowledge of China's underwater archaeology across the world, and make a contribution to the development of the discipline in China.

Reference

1.Ningbo Municipal Institute of Cultural Relics and Archaeology and Ningbo Base, National Center of Underwater Cultural Heritage. 2014. *Underwater Archaeology in China Exhibition Outline.* Unpublished.

2.Wang Jiehua, Ningbo Municipal Institute of Cultural Relics and Archaeology, Ningbo Base, National Center of Underwater Cultural Heritage, 2014. *Sixteen Years' Journey—Retrospect and Prospect of Underwater Archaeology in Ningbo.China Cultural Relics News,* 26 Sept. p. 5.

3.Wang Jiehua, 2014, *Ten Years' Preparation for One Excavation— Discuss Ningbo Underwater Archaeology from the Case of "Xiaobaijiao Ⅰ" Shipwreck Excavation.* In: National Center of Underwater Cultural Heritage, Ningbo Municipal Institute of Cultural Relics and Archaeology eds., 2014. *24 Meters Underwater—The Documentary of "Xiaobaijiao Ⅰ" Underwater Archaeological Project in Xiangshan County of Ningbo.* Beijing: China Radio Film & TV Press. P 150-162.

4.Lin Guocong, Wang Jiehua from Ningbo Municipal Institute of Cultural Relics and Archaeology, Jiang Bo from National Center of Underwater Cultural Heritage, 2014. *Another Innovation Work of Underwater Archaeology in China—2014 Excavation of Shipwreck "Xiaobaijiao Ⅰ" in Ningbo, Zhejiang Province, China Cultural Relics News,* 29 Aug. p. 5.

5.Lou Hongbin, Wang Jiehua from Ningbo Municipal Institute of Cultural Relics and Archaeology, Feng Yi from China Port Museum, National Center of Underwater Cultural Heritage, 2014. *The Review of the Establishment and Construction of the China Port Museum and Ningbo Base, National Center of Underwater Cultural Heritage. China Cultural Relics News,* 10 Oct. p. 6-7.

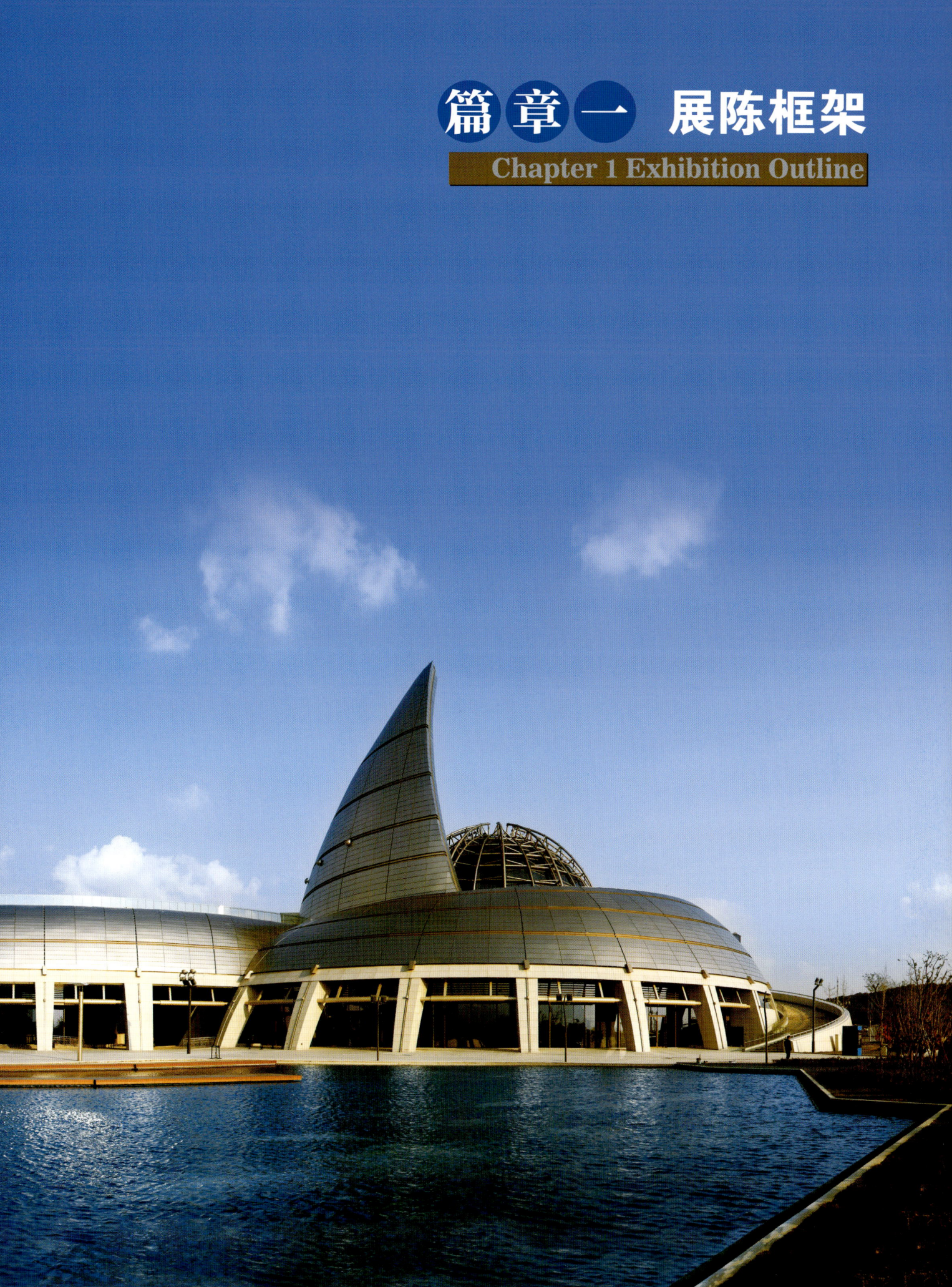

篇章一 展陈框架
Chapter 1 Exhibition Outline

前 言

中国水下考古肇始于20世纪80年代。1986年7月,我国首次水下考古工作座谈会在京召开,讨论了制定水下文物保护法规与建立水下考古机构问题。1987年,由国家文物局牵头成立了"国家水下考古协调小组",随后在原中国历史博物馆建立了我国第一个水下考古专业机构。此后20多年间,国家和地方不断强化投入与支持力度,极大推动了水下考古在中国的发展。特别是2009年国家文物局水下文化遗产保护中心组建以来,我国的水下考古逐步向水下文化遗产保护方向转变,工作领域亦逐步从近海扩展到远海和内陆水域,"国家主导,部门协作,地方参与"的水下文化遗产保护格局开始逐步形成。

今天,我们在这里隆重推出"水下考古在中国"专题陈列,旨在推进水下考古知识的公众普及、水下考古成果的社会共享和水下考古工作的深入发展。今后,随着国家综合实力的不断增强,我们相信,我国的水下考古事业将会迎来更加辉煌的明天。

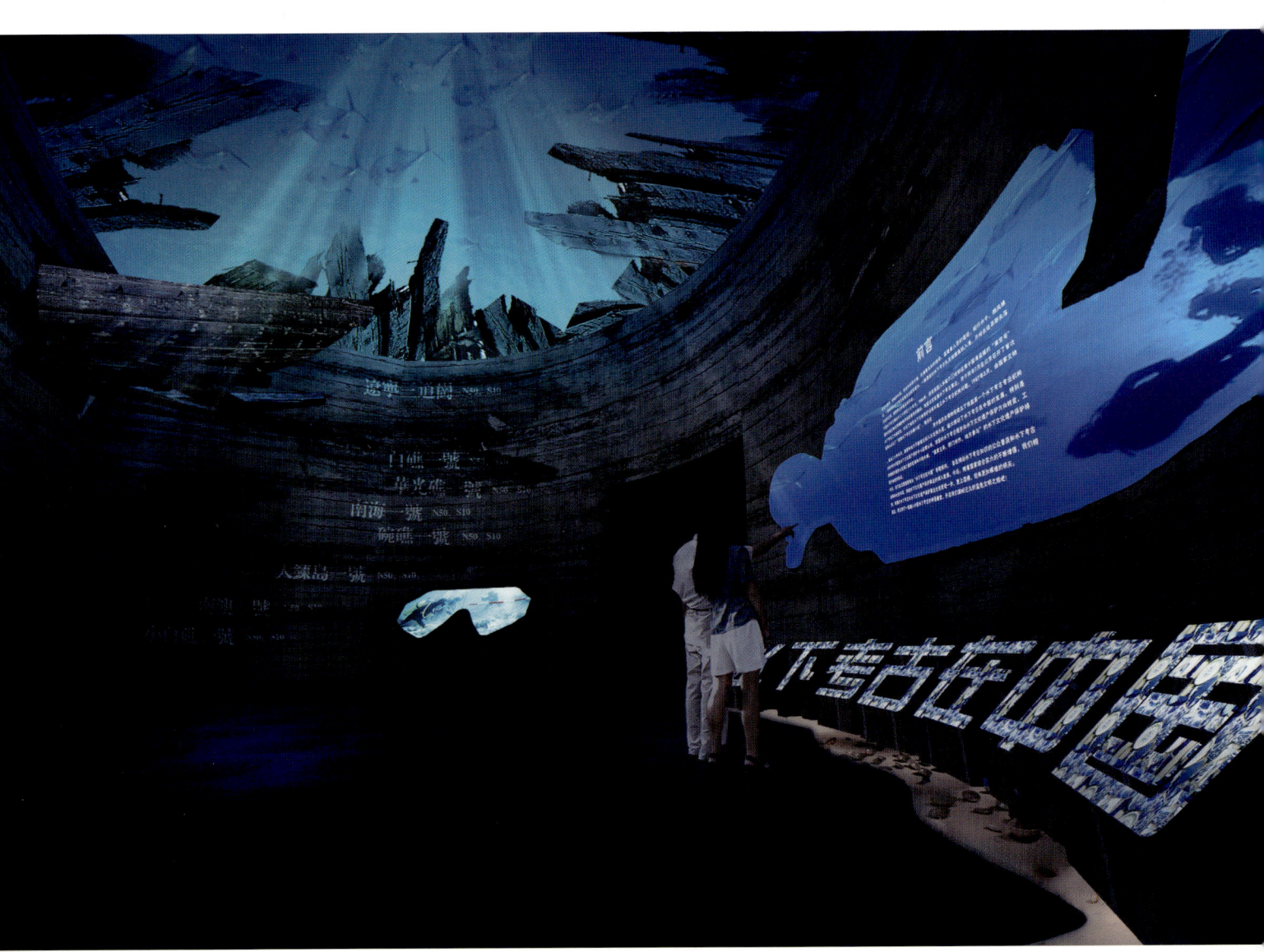

Preface

Chinese underwater archaeology was established in the early 1980s. In July of 1986, the first Chinese underwater archaeology symposium was held in Beijing. This symposium proposed laws and regulations to preserve China's underwater remains and relics, which ultimately led to the Chinese Underwater Archaeological Institute. In 1987, the National Underwater Archaeological Group was established after its proposal by the State Administration of Cultural Heritage. Based on this group, the Chinese Underwater Archaeological Institute was established at the National Museum of China. Over the following two decades, the field of China's underwater archaeology gradually developed under the support and supervision of China's central and provincial governments. Following the establishment of the National Center of Underwater Cultural Heritage of the State Administration of Cultural Heritage in 2009, China's underwater archaeology changed its focus to protect China's underwater relics and heritage. Fieldwork extended from the coastal areas to deep seas and inland waters. The study principle of "leading by government, supporting by institute, and participating with local authorities" was proposed to start protecting China's underwater heritage.

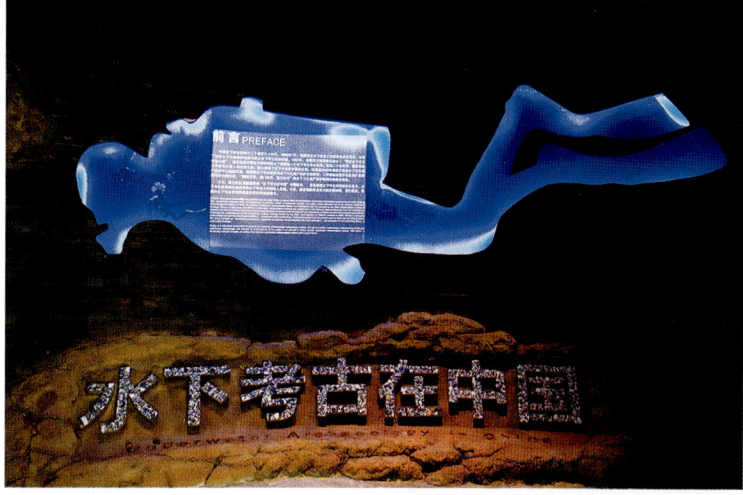

Today, it is with great honour that we present the exhibition of *Underwater Archaeology in China*. We aim to provide a professional understanding of China's underwater archaeology and present its achievements to the public in an attempt to further current underwater archaeological studies. With China's increasing national strength, we believe that Chinese underwater archaeological studies will have a great future.

机构与队伍

在国家文物局的积极推动下，1987年，我国第一个水下考古专业机构——原中国历史博物馆水下考古学研究室（现中国国家博物馆水下考古研究中心）挂牌成立，自此拉开了我国水下考古的历史序幕；2009年，国家文物局水下文化遗产保护中心正式组建，由此揭开了我国水下考古的崭新篇章。

20多年来，我国还相继在浙江、广东、福建、海南、山东、湖北等地建立了区域性、地方性水下考古机构，在国内外举办了多次水下考古、出水文物科技保护和技术潜水培训，水下文化遗产保护机构布局日臻完善，专业队伍日趋壮大，已成为我国水下考古与水下文化遗产保护最中坚的技术力量。

Institutes and Staff

Supported by the State Administration of Cultural Heritage, the first China's underwater archaeological institute was established in 1987, as the Underwater Archaeology Department of the Chinese History Museum (now the Underwater Archaeological Research Centre of the National Museum of China). This marks the beginning of China's underwater archaeological studies. In 2009, the State Administration of Cultural Heritage established the Underwater Cultural Heritage Centre, marking a new era in China's underwater archaeology.

Over the last 20 years, provincial underwater archaeological institutes have been established in many provinces, including Zhejiang, Guangdong, Fujian, Hainan, Shandong and Hubei. Professional training courses have been offered, with courses in underwater archaeology, archaeological preservation and diving technology. Thanks to the efforts of local authorities, the provincial underwater archaeological institutes are well developed. Experts and archaeologists of academic achievements have been introduced to improve underwater archaeology and preservation techniques of China's underwater heritage.

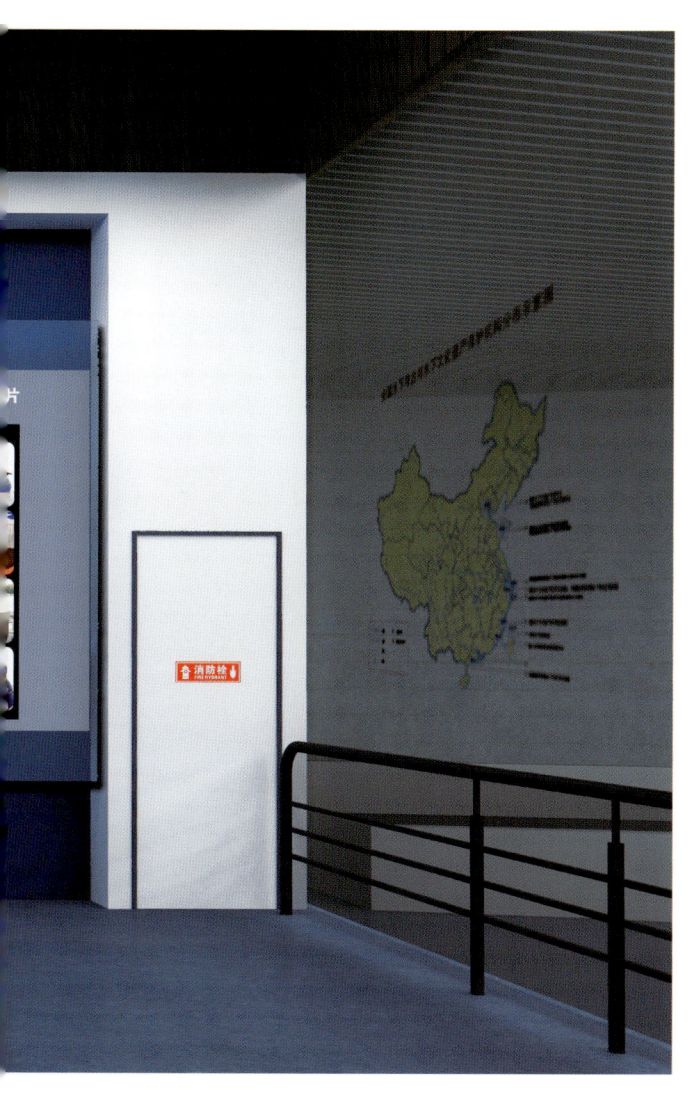

技术与方法

水下考古是一门有机融合了现代科学技术和传统考古方法的新兴学科。神游海底是人类由来已久的愿望，人类一直渴望能够如鱼儿般畅游水中，科学技术的进步和潜水设备的发明，终使人类探索海底世界奥秘、追寻蓝色海洋文明的梦想成真。

20多年来，我国水下考古的技术方法不断创新，工作流程逐步完善，潜水、探测、测绘、摄影、摄像、通讯、定位、监控、保护、水下考古机器人、水下考古专用船等现代科技装备的陆续应用，以及《水下考古工作规程》的颁布试行，有力推动了我国水下考古与水下文化遗产保护工作的向前发展。

Techniques and Methodologies

Underwater archaeology is a new subject that systematically combines modern science and traditional archaeology. Humans have always dreamed of being able to explore the unknown of the great blue ocean world by swimming like fish, and improvements in scientific techniques and diving equipment have now made the dream come true.

Over the past 20 years, Chinese underwater archaeological techniques and methodologies have greatly improved. Systematic, step-by-step working guidelines have been instituted. New modern scientific equipment has been applied involving diving, detecting, drawing, photographing, camera shooting, communicating, position locating, video surveying, and preserving by using Remote Operated Vehicle and specially designed working boats. The promulgation of *Regulations of Underwater Archaeological Work* also further pushed the development of China's underwater archaeology.

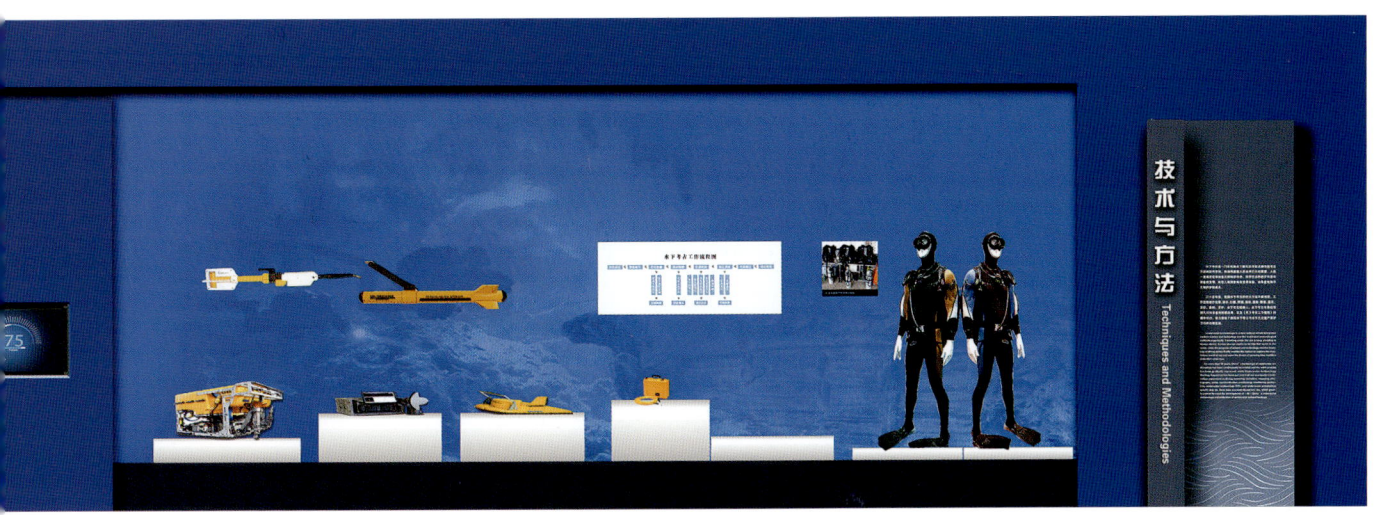

篇章一　展陈框架
Chapter 1 Exhibition Outline

调查与发掘

在国家各部委与国家文物局的重视支持,以及各个水下考古专业机构和各地文物行政部门的携手努力下,我国已相继在南海、东海、黄海、渤海海域及部分内陆水域开展了一系列卓有成效的水下考古调查、探测、探摸、发掘工作,共发现重要水下文化遗存数百处,初步摸清了我国水下文化遗产的家底。

20多年来,以"南海Ⅰ号"、"华光礁Ⅰ号"、"半洋礁Ⅰ号"、绥中元代沉船、"南澳Ⅰ号"、"碗礁Ⅰ号"、"小白礁Ⅰ号"为代表的古代沉船遗址和以"中山舰"为代表的近现代水下文化遗存的抢救发掘,以及以南沙群岛、均州古城为代表的水下文化遗产资源调查,均取得了丰硕成果,引起了广泛关注。

Surveys and Excavations

With the full support of the China's central government and State Administration of Cultural Heritage, and deeply through joint work with professional underwater archaeological institutes and provincial cultural heritage departments, the China's underwater archaeology institutes undertook and completed a series of remarkable studies, including surveys of underwater remains, scientific tests, and excavations in the South China Sea, the East China Sea, the Huanghai Sea and the Bohai Sea, as well as in some inland waters. Hundreds of remains and sites have been discovered, which has allowed for a good understanding of the distribution of Chinese underwater relics.

Over the last 20 years, the Chinese underwater archaeological institutes have conducted such salvage excavations as the ancient shipwrecks of Nanhai Ⅰ, Huaguangjiao Ⅰ, Banyangjiao Ⅰ, Suizhong Yuan Dynasty Shipwreck, Nan'ao Ⅰ, Wanjiao Ⅰ, and Xiao Baijiao Ⅰ; as the early modern period shipwreck of Zhongshan Warship. The institutes have also undertaken underwater archaeological surveys in the Spratly Islands and the inland underwater remains of Junzhou City. These works represent a series of the latest excellent Chinese underwater archaeological studies of great importance to both China and the world.

规划与展望

我国拥有近300万平方千米的辽阔海域、1.8万多千米的海岸线和丰富的内陆水域，水下文化遗产数量巨大、种类多样。开展水下考古，保护好、研究好、利用好这些珍贵的水下文化遗产，是传承中华海洋文明、推动文化大发展、大繁荣的内在要求，也是实施国家海洋战略、维护国家安全利益的重要依据。

回首过去，一代又一代中国水下考古人付出了艰辛努力，取得了丰厚成果，赢得了广泛认同。展望未来，随着综合国力的增强、各级政府的重视和社会各界的支持，我国水下考古与水下文化遗产保护事业必将勾画出更加美好的宏伟蓝图！

Plans and Expectations

China's vast sea territory covers nearly 3 million square kilometres, with an 18,000-kilometer coastline, rich resources of inland waters and countless variations in underwater relics. Underwater archaeological studies should meet internal requirements that adhere to the proper maintenance, study, and application of underwater heritage policies, and become an important base of national maritime strategies and national interest protection.

Looking back at the past, generations of archaeologists have devoted their best efforts to the archiving and development of the fruitful field of Chinese underwater archaeology. A great number of monographs, archaeological achievements and studies have been accepted on an international scale. Looking ahead, with China's increasing overall national strength, by the leadership and concern of all levels of governments and the support of the public and cooperative institutes, China's underwater archaeology and the great cause of China's underwater cultural heritage will have a bright future.

在宁波基地陈列展示区内，还设有专门的沉船修复展示室。这里既是"水下考古在中国"专题陈列的一个特别展区，也是"小白礁Ⅰ号"保护修复的工作场所。公众透过通电玻璃，可以直观欣赏到古代沉船的保护场景与修复流程。

The Shipwreck Conservation Area located in the Display Area of Ningbo Base, National Center of Underwater Cultural Heritage ia not only a special section in *Underwater Archaeology in China* Exhibition, but also a laboratory of "Xiaobaijiao Ⅰ" shipwreck conservation. Visitors could learn the process of ancient shipwreck preservation through the switchable glass.

规划与展望

我国拥有近300万平方千米的辽阔海域、1.8万多千米的海岸线和丰富的内陆水域，水下文化遗产数量巨大、种类多样。开展水下考古，保护好、研究好、利用好这些珍贵的水下文化遗产，是传承中华海洋文明、推动文化大发展、大繁荣的内在要求，也是实施国家海洋战略、维护国家安全利益的重要依据。

回首过去，一代又一代中国水下考古人付出了艰辛努力，取得了丰厚成果，赢得了广泛认同。展望未来，随着综合国力的增强、各级政府的重视和社会各界的支持，我国水下考古与水下文化遗产保护事业必将勾画出更加美好的宏伟蓝图！

Plans and Expectations

China's vast sea territory covers nearly 3 million square kilometres, with an 18,000-kilometer coastline, rich resources of inland waters and countless variations in underwater relics. Underwater archaeological studies should meet internal requirements that adhere to the proper maintenance, study, and application of underwater heritage policies, and become an important base of national maritime strategies and national interest protection.

Looking back at the past, generations of archaeologists have devoted their best efforts to the archiving and development of the fruitful field of Chinese underwater archaeology. A great number of monographs, archaeological achievements and studies have been accepted on an international scale. Looking ahead, with China's increasing overall national strength, by the leadership and concern of all levels of governments and the support of the public and cooperative institutes, China's underwater archaeology and the great cause of China's underwater cultural heritage will have a bright future.

Surveys and Excavations

With the full support of the China's central government and State Administration of Cultural Heritage, and deeply through joint work with professional underwater archaeological institutes and provincial cultural heritage departments, the China's underwater archaeology institutes undertook and completed a series of remarkable studies, including surveys of underwater remains, scientific tests, and excavations in the South China Sea, the East China Sea, the Huanghai Sea and the Bohai Sea, as well as in some inland waters. Hundreds of remains and sites have been discovered, which has allowed for a good understanding of the distribution of Chinese underwater relics.

Over the last 20 years, the Chinese underwater archaeological institutes have conducted such salvage excavations as the ancient shipwrecks of Nanhai Ⅰ, Huaguangjiao Ⅰ, Banyangjiao Ⅰ, Suizhong Yuan Dynasty Shipwreck, Nan'ao Ⅰ, Wanjiao Ⅰ, and Xiao Baijiao Ⅰ; as the early modern period shipwreck of Zhongshan Warship. The institutes have also undertaken underwater archaeological surveys in the Spratly Islands and the inland underwater remains of Junzhou City. These works represent a series of the latest excellent Chinese underwater archaeological studies of great importance to both China and the world.

保护与交流

我国在开创和推进水下考古事业的进程中,始终坚持调查与发掘并举、抢救与保护并重的宗旨,切实推动水下文物法律法规建设,持续举办出水文物科技保护培训,全面开展海洋文化遗产联合执法行动,积极探索建立水下文化遗产监控体系,为我国水下文化遗产的保护和海洋文化战略的实施作出了重要贡献。

二十多年来,随着我国综合国力和水下考古实力的不断增强,中国水下考古人的身影开始频频出现在国际水下考古的大舞台上。涉外性水下考古调查项目的连续实施,国际性水下考古工作会议的应邀参与,高规格水下考古学术研讨会议的联合召开,以及一大批水下考古科研成果的出版发行,无不昭示着我国水下考古正向着系统化、科学化和国际化全方位转变。

Preservation and Communication

The China's underwater archaeology institutes have contributed tremendously to the preservation of China's underwater cultural heritage and the implementation of national maritime cultural strategy through the development of China's underwater archaeological studies: by adherence to strategies equally stressing both excavations and surveys, as well as equally emphasising both salvage and preservation; through the construction and thorough implementation of the laws of underwater relics; by offering professional training in the preservation techniques of underwater objects; by extensive joint actions regarding maritime cultural heritage; by exploring new systems for undertaking the supervision of China's underwater cultural heritage.

Over the past 20 years, as China has grown in overall national strength, many Chinese archaeologists have stepped onto the world stage of underwater archaeological studies. Involvement in foreign archaeological projects, participation in international academic conferences, holding high-level underwater archaeological symposiums, and many seminal publications in underwater archaeological research fully indicate that China's underwater archaeology is developing toward an all-encompassing approach to a systematised, scientific, and globalised archaeology.

篇章二 展陈文物
Chapter 2 Exhibition Artefacts

"南海Ⅰ号"南宋沉船
Southern Song Dynasty Shipwreck "Nanhai Ⅰ"

"南海Ⅰ号"南宋沉船遗址位于广东台山市上川岛、下川岛附近海域，1987年发现，2001至2004年进行勘探、试掘，2007年成功实施了世界首创的整体沉箱打捞，代表了当前我国水下考古的最高水平。已出水文物以瓷器为主，包括德化窑、磁灶窑、景德镇窑系及龙泉窑系的高质量精品。现存广东海上丝绸之路博物馆。

The Southern Song Dynasty shipwreck "Nanhai Ⅰ" is located under the sea near Shangchuan and Xiachuan Islands, Taishan City, Guangdong Province. The ship remains were discovered in 1987. The initial surveys and exploratory excavations were carried out from 2001 to 2004. In 2007, the shipwreck was successfully excavated by means of a steel caisson encasing the entire remains and surrounding mud, which is a technique pioneered by the Chinese and at the cutting edge of China's underwater archaeology. The objects unearthed were mainly fine ceramics, including Dehua wares, Cizao ceramics, Jingdezhen porcelains, and Longquan celadons. These artefacts are now housed at the Maritime Silk Road Museum of Guangdong.

龙泉窑青釉划花碗
Longquan Kiln Celadon Bowl Incised with Floral Design

2002NHIT2019:1097

口径19.2cm　底径6.3cm　高7.6cm

Diameter at Rim 19.2cm　Diameter at Footring 6.3cm　Height 7.6cm

广东海上丝绸之路博物馆　藏

Maritime Silk Road Museum of Guangdong Collection

敞口，斜弧腹，圈足。灰胎，胎体厚重，胎质坚硬。青釉，青中泛黄，足底无釉。内腹壁和内底刻画莲花纹。

（撰稿：田国敏）

闽清义窑青白釉划花碗

Fujian Qingyi Kiln Blue and White Glazed Bowl Incised with Floral Design

2002NHIT2018:300

口径18.1cm 底径6.2cm 高6.5cm

Diameter at Rim 18.1cm Diameter at Footring 6.2cm Height 6.5cm

广东海上丝绸之路博物馆 藏

Maritime Silk Road Museum of Guangdong Collection

　　花口外撇，斜弧腹，圈足。青白釉，足底无釉。内腹壁和内底刻画花卉纹，构图简练，线条清晰。

（撰稿：田国敏）

景德镇窑青白釉婴戏纹碗

Jingdezhen Kiln Blue and White Glazed Bowl with Children Playing Design

2002NHIT2019：430

口径20.6cm　底径5.8cm　高5.7cm

Diameter at Rim 20.6cm　Diameter at Footring 5.8cm　Height 5.7cm

广东海上丝绸之路博物馆　藏

Maritime Silk Road Museum of Guangdong Collection

敞口，斜弧腹，圈足。白胎，胎体较薄，胎质坚硬，青白釉，足底无釉。内腹壁和内底刻画婴儿戏莲纹。　　　　（撰稿：田国敏）

景德镇窑青白釉印花葵口碟
Jingdezhen Kiln Blue and White Glazed Dish with Floral Petal-shaped Rim Impressed with Floral Design

2009NHIT0938
口径14.4cm　底径3.8cm　高3.3cm
Diameter at Rim 14.4cm　Diameter at Footring 3.8cm　Height 3.3cm
广东海上丝绸之路博物馆　藏
Maritime Silk Road Museum of Guangdong Collection

　　葵口外撇，斜腹，圈足较矮。白胎较薄，胎质细密。青白釉，釉色光亮莹润，施釉至足底。内腹壁模印莲花纹，碟心一圈弦纹，内印花枝纹。

（撰稿：田国敏）

磁灶窑绿釉印花碟

Cizao Kiln Green Glazed Dish Impressed with Floral Design

2010NHI2010：100

口径10.7cm　底径5.8cm　高1.8cm

Diameter at Rim 10.7cm　Diameter at Footring 5.8cm　Height 1.8cm

广东海上丝绸之路博物馆　藏

Maritime Silk Road Museum of Guangdong Collection

菱口，宽沿，浅弧腹，平底。灰胎，胎质较粗。通体绿釉。口沿沿面模印缠枝花卉纹，内底模印葡萄纹。

（撰稿：田国敏）

磁灶窑酱釉扁罐
Cizao Kiln Brown Glazed Jar

2004NHIC13: 2

口径3.1cm　底径8.8cm　腹径12.6cm　高8.1cm

Diameter at Rim 3.1cm　Diameter at Footring 8.8cm

Widest Diameter 12.6cm　Height 8.1cm

广东海上丝绸之路博物馆　藏

Maritime Silk Road Museum of Guangdong Collection

　　平口，溜肩，鼓腹，平底。灰胎，胎质较粗。酱釉，釉至下腹。外底墨书"林□"。①

（撰稿：田国敏）

① 此处用"□"表示分辨不清的字符。全书同。

磁灶窑酱釉四系罐
Cizao Kiln Brown Glazed Jar with Four Rings

2004NHIC2:2

口径9.4cm 底径9.7cm 腹径17.6cm 高20.1cm

Diameter at Rim 9.4cm　Diameter at Footring 9.7cm

Widest Diameter 17.6cm　Height 20.1cm

广东海上丝绸之路博物馆　藏

Maritime Silk Road Museum of Guangdong Collection

　　唇口，短颈，溜肩，四耳，鼓腹，平底。酱釉，釉至下腹。外底墨书"囗"。

（撰稿：田国敏）

德化窑青白釉印花双系罐
Dehua Kiln Blue and White Glazed Jar with Double Rings Impressed with Floral Design

2002NHIT2020: 638

口径2.1cm　底径3.2cm　腹径6.0cm　高7.7cm

Diameter at Rim 2.1cm　Diameter at Footring 3.2cm　Widest Diameter 6.0cm　Height 7.7cm

广东海上丝绸之路博物馆　藏
Maritime Silk Road Museum of Guangdong Collection

　　敛口，双管状系，溜肩，鼓腹，平底。白胎，胎质细密。青白釉，外底露胎。上下腹壁各模印两圈弦纹和缠枝花卉纹。

（撰稿：田国敏）

德化窑青白釉葫芦瓶

Dehua Kiln Blue and White Glazed Gourd Vase

2007NHIC6：4

口径1.1cm 底径3.8cm 高8.7cm

Diameter at Rim 1.1cm   Diameter at Footring 3.8cm   Height 8.7cm

广东海上丝绸之路博物馆 藏

Maritime Silk Road Museum of Guangdong Collection

平口，葫芦状，矮饼足。白胎，胎质细密。青白釉，外底露胎。器表有粘接痕。

（撰稿：田国敏）

德化窑青白釉印花喇叭口瓶

Dehua Kiln Blue and White Glazed Vase with Horn-shaped Rim Impressed with Floral Design

2002NHIT2019：1133

口径4.9cm　底径5.3cm　腹径5.6cm　高9.8cm

Diameter at Rim 4.9cm　Diameter at Footring 5.3cm　Widest Diameter 5.6cm　Height 9.8cm

广东海上丝绸之路博物馆　藏

Maritime Silk Road Museum of Guangdong Collection

　　撇口，束颈，鼓腹，圈足外撇，呈喇叭状。白胎，胎质细密。青白釉，外底露胎。腹壁及足面模印莲瓣纹。器表有粘接痕。

（撰稿：田国敏）

德化窑青白釉粉盒

Dehua Kiln Blue and White Glazed Cosmetic Box

2002NHIT2019: 611（盖） 2002NHIT2019: 276（底）

口径7.0cm 底径5.6cm 高5.6cm

Diameter at Rim 7.0cm　Diameter at Footring 5.6cm　Height 5.6cm

广东海上丝绸之路博物馆　藏

Maritime Silk Road Museum of Guangdong Collection

器盖圆鼓，子母口，斜直腹，平底微内凹。白胎，胎质细密。青白釉，外底露胎。外底墨书"百"字，字迹潦草。

（撰稿：田国敏）

铜环
Bronze Ring

2007NHIL15
外径8.6cm　内径7.3cm
Outer Diameter 8.6cm　Inner Diameter 7.3cm
广东海上丝绸之路博物馆　藏
Maritime Silk Road Museum of Guangdong Collection

铜质。圆环状。器表发黑，有铜绿。　　　　（撰稿：田国敏）

"半洋礁 I 号"南宋沉船
Southern Song Dynasty Shipwreck "Banyangjiao I"

"半洋礁 I 号"南宋沉船遗址位于福建省龙海市隆教畲族乡东南半洋暗礁海域，发现于2010年。船体方向330度，残长约9.2米、宽约2.5米，见有船舷板、部分船底板、船桅座、龙骨等。遗物主要为黑釉盏、少量印花青白瓷碗片、陶盆、陶壶等，较特别的遗物有石质碗片、铜刀镡（格）、锡碗、漆木片等。

The Southern Song Dynasty shipwreck "Banyangjiao I" is located in Banyangjiao Sea, southeast to Shezu Village in Longjiao, Longhai City, Fujian Province. It was found in 2010, with the body oriented in 330 degree, the remaining part of the wreck length of 9.2 meters and width of 2.5 meters. The remains still preserved the ship structures such as bulwark, part of the bottom board, mast base, and keel. The artefacts found inside the ship were mainly black glazed wares, few sherds of impressed blue and white porcelains, pottery basins, jars, and some special findings including fragments of stone wares, copper knives, tin wares, lacquer wares, etc.

福清东张窑黑釉兔毫盏
Fuqing Dongzhang Kiln Small Cup with Hare's Fur Glaze

LB1311

口径10.7cm　底径3.4cm　高5.6cm

Diameter at Rim 10.7cm　Diameter at Footring 3.4cm　Height 5.6cm

龙海市博物馆　藏

Longhai Museum Collection

　　侈口，斜直腹略内收，圈足，足底有割胚痕。灰胎，胎质坚硬，胎体粗糙，可见砂粒。酱黑釉，釉至下腹，腹底积釉，釉层较厚；釉面有黄褐色毫丝，呈辐射状。

（撰稿：林国聪、张红兴）

篇章二 展陈文物
Chapter 2 Exhibition Artefacts

福清东张窑黑釉盏
Fuqing Dongzhang Kiln Black Glazed Small Cup

LB1060

口径11.1cm 底径3.6cm 高5.7cm

Diameter at Rim 11.1cm　Diameter at Footring 3.6cm　Height 5.7cm

龙海市博物馆　藏

Longhai Museum Collection

侈口，斜直腹略内收，圈足。灰胎，胎质坚硬，胎体粗糙，可见砂粒。酱黑釉，釉至下腹，腹底积釉，釉层较厚，釉面光亮。

（撰稿：林国聪、张红兴）

福建青白釉花卉纹芒口碗

Fujian Blue and White Glazed Bowl with Unglazed Rim and Flowers Design

LB1278

口径7.5cm　底径4.2cm　高5.7cm

Diameter at Rim 7.5cm　Diameter at Footring 4.2cm　Height 5.7cm

龙海市博物馆　藏

Longhai Museum Collection

芒口，敞口，斜直腹下弧，圈足较矮。腹部有一道裂痕。白胎，胎质细密且坚硬。青白釉，施釉至足底。釉层较薄，釉色光亮莹润。内腹壁模印云雷纹边饰条带，其下六开光莲纹，内底饰两折枝花。

（撰稿：林国聪、张红兴）

福建青白釉花卉双鱼纹芒口碗

Fujian Blue and White Glazed Bowl with Unglazed Rim and Flowers and Fishes Design

LB1288

口径15.0cm　底径4.7cm　高6.8cm

Diameter at Rim 15.0cm　Diameter at Footring 4.7cm　Height 6.8cm

龙海市博物馆　藏

Longhai Museum Collection

　　芒口外撇，斜直腹下弧，圈足较矮。腹部有一道裂痕。白胎，胎质细密且坚硬。青白釉，釉至足底。釉层较薄，釉色光亮莹润。内腹壁模印六开光花卉纹，内底模印双鱼纹。　　（撰稿：林国聪、张红兴）

福建青白釉婴戏纹芒口碗
Fujian Blue and White Glazed Bowl with Unglazed Rim and Children Playing Design

LB1287

口径14.7cm　底径4.0cm　高5.6cm

Diameter at Rim 14.7cm　Diameter at Footring 4.0cm　Height 5.6cm

龙海市博物馆　藏

Longhai Museum Collection

　　芒口外撇，斜弧腹，圈足。白胎，胎质细密且坚硬。青白釉，釉至足底。釉层较薄，釉色光亮莹润。内腹壁模印一周乳突，其下饰两组婴儿戏莲纹，内底下凹。

（撰稿：林国聪、张红兴）

福清东张窑褐釉草叶纹盆
Fuqing Dongzhang Kiln Brown Glazed Basin with Leaves Design

LB1015
口径20.1cm 底径15.5cm 高5.7cm
Diameter at Rim 20.1cm　Diameter at Footring 15.5cm　Height 5.7cm
龙海市博物馆　藏
Longhai Museum Collection

　　圆唇，敛口，弧腹，平底。器表有裂痕。灰褐陶，质坚硬，胎粗糙。褐釉，外底露胎。内底较平，彩绘褐色草叶纹。

（撰稿：林国聪、张红兴）

绥中三道岗元代沉船
Yuan Dynasty Suizhong Sandaogang Shipwreck

绥中元代沉船遗址位于辽宁绥中三道岗海域，1992年至1997年发掘，是我国首次独立完成的水下考古发掘项目。出水遗物共600余件，以陶瓷器为主，大多为磁州窑产的白地黑釉罐、盆等。

The Yuan Dynasty shipwreck is located in the Sandaogang Sea of Suizhong County of Liaoning Province. The shipwreck was excavated from 1992 to 1997 and was the first underwater archaeological excavation accomplished using only Chinese archaeologists and techniques. About 600 objects were excavated, mainly ceramic sand porcelains. Most of these were black glazed jars and basins made in Cizhou Kiln.

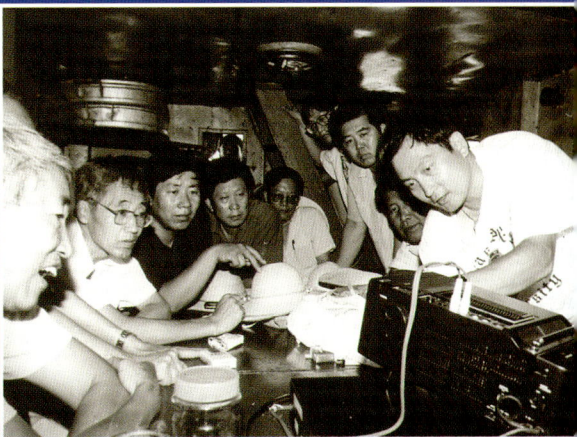

磁州窑白釉褐彩鱼藻纹盆
Cizhou Kiln White Glazed Basin with a Fish in a Pond in Brown Pigment

HB1008

口径38.8cm　底径18.8cm　高15.5cm

Diameter at Rim 38.8cm　Diameter at Footring 18.8cm　Height 15.5cm

葫芦岛市博物馆　藏

Huludao Museum Collection

  圆唇，宽沿外折，沿唇稍下翻，斜直腹，平底微内凹。白胎泛黄，胎体厚重。沿面与器内施白色化妆土，外罩透明釉；外腹中部施酱黑釉，宽带状，上缘整齐，下缘垂釉；口沿外侧、外腹底部及外底露胎。沿面饰草叶连点纹，内腹壁饰四周粗弦纹与辐射状水波纹，盆心饰两周弦纹，内饰鱼藻纹；外底中部浅挖。　　　　（撰稿：林国聪、王光远）

磁州窑白釉褐彩花草纹罐
Cizhou Kiln White Glazed Jar with Floral Design in Brown Pigment

HB1003

口径10.6cm　底径7.2cm　高12.5cm

Diameter at Rim 10.6cm　Diameter at Footring 7.2cm　Height 12.5cm

葫芦岛市博物馆　藏

Huludao Museum Collection

　　直口，方沿，弧肩，上腹鼓，下腹斜内收，足底内凹。白胎泛黄，胎体厚重。白色化妆土，外罩透明釉；内外满釉。肩部饰一周连点纹条带，腹部有两处菱形开光，内绘花卉，开光之间上下相对饰草叶纹样；近底处饰一周弦纹。

（撰稿：林国聪、王光远）

磁州窑白釉褐彩龙凤纹罐

Cizhou Kiln White Glazed Jar with Dragon and Phoenix Design in Brown Pigment

HB0481

口径18.6cm　底径11.6cm　高30.0cm

Diameter at Rim 18.6cm　Diameter at Footring 11.6cm　Height 30.0cm

葫芦岛市博物馆　藏

Huludao Museum Collection

　　方唇，直口，溜肩，上腹鼓，下腹斜直内收，足底内凹。白胎泛黄，胎体厚重。白色化妆土，外罩透明釉；内外满釉，外底露胎。肩部上下两组弦纹，内绘缠枝菊花纹；腹部有两处菱形开光，内分别绘一游龙、一飞凤，龙凤在云气衬托中，或张牙舞爪，或展翅飞翔，在开光间绘折枝花卉。　　　　　　（撰稿：林国聪、王光远）

磁州窑黑白釉草叶纹碗
Cizhou Kiln Black and White Glazed Bowl with Leaves Design

HB0675

口径19.0cm　底径6.9cm　高9.8cm

Diameter at Rim 19.0cm　Diameter at Footring 6.9cm　Height 9.8cm

葫芦岛市博物馆　藏

Huludao Museum Collection

　　敞口，斜直腹下弧，圈足较矮。器表有裂痕。白胎泛黄，胎体厚重。碗内及外腹上部施白色化妆土，外罩透明釉，釉面开裂片；外腹中部以下施酱黑釉，外腹底部及外底露胎。内腹壁釉下饰三周褐色弦纹，碗心饰彩绘褐色草叶纹。

（撰稿：林国聪、王光远）

磁州窑黑白釉草叶纹碗

Cizhou Kiln Black and White Glazed Bowl with Leaves Design

HB0685

口径14.9cm　底径6.1cm　高6.9cm

Diameter at Rim 14.9cm　Diameter at Footring 6.1cm　Height 6.9cm

葫芦岛市博物馆　藏

Huludao Museum Collection

　　敞口，斜直腹下弧，圈足较矮。器表有裂痕。白胎泛黄，胎体厚重。碗内及外腹上部施白色化妆土，外罩透明釉，釉面开裂片；外腹中部以下施酱黑釉，外腹底部及外底露胎。内腹壁釉下饰三周褐色弦纹，碗心饰彩绘褐色草叶纹。

（撰稿：林国聪、王光远）

磁州窑黑白釉碗

Cizhou Kiln Black and White Glazed Bowl

HB0190

口径10.5cm 底径4.5cm 高4.0cm

Diameter at Rim 10.5cm   Diameter at Footring 4.5cm   Height 4.0cm

葫芦岛市博物馆 藏

Huludao Museum Collection

敞口，斜直腹下弧，圈足较矮。器表有裂痕。白胎泛黄，胎体厚重。碗内及外腹上部施白色化妆土，外罩透明釉；外腹下部及圈足施酱黑釉。

（撰稿：林国聪、王光远）

磁州窑黑釉菊瓣纹碗

Cizhou Kiln Black Glazed Bowl with Chrysanthemum Petals

HB0698

口径15.1cm　底径6.0cm　高6.9cm

Diameter at Rim 15.1cm　Diameter at Footring 6.0cm　Height 6.9cm

葫芦岛市博物馆　藏

Huludao Museum Collection

　　敞口，斜弧腹，圈足较矮。胎体厚重。碗内及外腹上部施酱黑釉，下腹至底附满铁锈色凝结物。内腹壁上下各彩绘一组褐色菊瓣纹，呈辐射状。

（撰稿：林国聪、王光远）

磁州窑黑釉菊瓣纹碗
Cizhou Kiln Black Glazed Bowl with Chrysanthemum Petals

HB0690

口径18.9cm　底径7.5cm　高9.5cm

Diameter at Rim 18.9cm　Diameter at Footring 7.5cm　Height 9.5cm

葫芦岛市博物馆　藏

Huludao Museum Collection

敞口，斜弧腹，圈足较矮。胎体厚重。碗内及外腹施酱黑釉，下腹至底露胎。内腹壁上下各彩绘一组褐色菊瓣纹，呈辐射状。

（撰稿：林国聪、王光远）

磁州窑白釉褐彩草叶纹器盖
Cizhou Kiln White Glazed Lid with Leaves Design in Brown Pigment

HB0723

口径12.5cm　沿径18.0cm　高6.0cm

Diameter at Rim 12.5cm　Diameter at Footring 18.0cm　Height 6.0cm

葫芦岛市博物馆　藏

Huludao Museum Collection

　　盖口圆唇，直口，弧壁；盖沿圆唇，宽平；盖面斜弧；盖顶圆饼状钮，钮面下凹。器表有裂痕。胎体较厚。盖外侧施白色化妆土，外罩透明釉，釉面开裂片；盖内侧露胎，胎表粗糙呈褐色。盖面两周弦纹之间饰三组草叶纹。

（撰稿：林国聪、王光远）

磁州窑白釉褐彩螺旋纹器盖
Cizhou Kiln White Glazed Lid with Spiral Design in Brown Pigment

HB0716

口径6.2cm　沿径10.2cm　高3.2cm
Diameter at Rim 6.2cm　Diameter at Footring 10.2cm　Height 3.2cm
葫芦岛市博物馆　藏
Huludao Museum Collection

　　盖口圆唇，直口，弧壁；盖沿圆唇，宽平；盖面圆鼓。白胎泛黄，胎体较厚。盖外侧施白色化妆土，外罩透明釉，釉面开裂片；盖内侧露胎。盖面釉下褐彩螺旋纹。器表有贝类附着物。　　　　（撰稿：林国聪、王光远）

磁州窑白釉褐彩草叶纹碟
Cizhou Kiln White Glazed Dish with Leaves Design in Brown Pigment

HB0649
口径13.6cm　底径6.7cm　高3.1cm
Diameter at Rim 13.6cm　Diameter at Footring 6.7cm　Height 3.1cm
葫芦岛市博物馆　藏
Huludao Museum Collection

　　圆唇，敛口，斜弧腹，矮圈足。白胎泛黄，胎体厚重。碗内及外腹上部施白色化妆土，外罩透明釉，釉面开裂片；外腹底部及外底露胎。内腹壁釉下饰两周褐色弦纹，盘心彩绘褐色草叶纹。　　　　（撰稿：林国聪、王光远）

磁州窑白釉褐彩草叶纹碟

Cizhou Kiln White Glazed Dish with Leaves Design in Brown Pigment

HB0646

口径14.4cm　底径7.0cm　高3.4cm

Diameter at Rim 14.4cm　Diameter at Footring 7.0cm　Height 3.4cm

葫芦岛市博物馆　藏

Huludao Museum Collection

　　圆唇，敛口，斜弧腹，矮圈足。白胎泛黄，胎体厚重。碗内及外腹上部施白色化妆土，外罩透明釉，釉面开裂片；外腹底部及外底露胎。内腹壁釉下饰两周褐色弦纹，盘心彩绘褐色草叶纹。

（撰稿：林国聪、王光远）

磁州窑白釉褐彩草叶纹碟
Cizhou Kiln White Glazed Dish with Leaves Design in Brown Pigment

HB0651

口径13.7cm　底径7.2cm　高3.1cm

Diameter at Rim 13.7cm　Diameter at Footring 7.2cm　Height 3.1cm

葫芦岛市博物馆　藏

Huludao Museum Collection

　　圆唇，敛口，斜弧腹，矮圈足。白胎泛黄，胎体厚重。碗内及外腹上部施白色化妆土，外罩透明釉，釉面开裂片；外腹底部及外底露胎。内腹壁釉下饰两周褐色弦纹，盘心彩绘褐色草叶纹。　　（撰稿：林国聪、王光远）

磁州窑白釉褐彩草叶纹碟
Cizhou Kiln White Glazed Dish with Leaves Design in Brown Pigment

HB0648

口径13.5cm　底径7.0cm　高3.1cm

Diameter at Rim 13.5cm　Diameter at Footring 7.0cm　Height 3.1cm

葫芦岛市博物馆　藏

Huludao Museum Collection

　　圆唇，敛口，斜弧腹，矮圈足。白胎泛黄，胎体厚重。碗内及外腹上部施白色化妆土，外罩透明釉，釉面开裂片；外腹底部及外底露胎。内腹壁釉下饰两周褐色弦纹，盘心彩绘褐色草叶纹。　　（撰稿：林国聪、王光远）

磁州窑白釉梅瓶
Cizhou Kiln White Glazed Vase

HB0109

口径4.8cm 底径9.1cm 高23.3cm

Diameter at Rim 4.8cm Diameter at Footring 9.1cm Height 23.3cm

葫芦岛市博物馆 藏

Huludao Museum Collection

  圆唇，喇叭口，短颈，丰肩，上腹微鼓，下腹斜直内收，凹底深挖。白胎泛黄，胎体厚重。瓶外壁施白色化妆土及透明釉，釉面开裂片；瓶内口沿处施酱黑釉。素面无纹。

（撰稿：林国聪、王光远）

篇章二 展陈文物
Chapter 2 Exhibition Artefacts

"南澳Ⅰ号"明代沉船
Ming Dynasty Shipwreck "Nan'ao Ⅰ"

"南澳Ⅰ号"明代沉船遗址位于广东汕头南澳海域，2007年发现，2010至2012年连续三年实施发掘，出水遗物近3万件，以青花瓷器为主，兼及陶器、铁器、锡器、火炮、铜钱、动植物遗存等，是我国水下考古的又一重大发现。现原址保护于南澳海域。

The Ming Dynasty shipwreck "Nan'ao Ⅰ" is located at Nan'ao Sea of Shantou in Guangdong Province. The ship remains was first discovered in 2007. From 2010 to 2012, three excavations have been carried out. The "Nan'ao Ⅰ" shipwreck is one of the most significant discoveries in Chinese underwater archaeology, as nearly 30,000 objects have been excavated with a majority of blue-and-white porcelains, and the rest include potteries, iron-works, tin-works, guns, coins and animal and plant remains. The shipwrecks have been preserved in site at Nan'ao Sea.

景德镇青花弦纹碗
Jingdezhen Kiln Blue-and-white Bowl with String Pattern

2010NANⅡ0103
口径17.2cm 底径6.2cm 高6.7cm
Diameter at Rim 17.2cm Diameter at Footring 6.2cm Height 6.7cm
国家文物局水下文化遗产保护中心 藏
National Center of Underwater Cultural Heritage Collection

敞口，弧腹，圈足。内外满釉，内底涩圈，足底露胎。内外腹壁上、下均饰有弦纹。（撰稿：王光远、史伟）

景德镇青花弦纹碗
Jingdezhen Kiln Blue-and-white Bowl with String Pattern

2011NASⅢ0107

口径17.6cm　底径6.2cm　高6.4cm

Diameter at Rim 17.6cm　Diameter at Footring 6.2cm　Height 6.4cm

国家文物局水下文化遗产保护中心　藏

National Center of Underwater Cultural Heritage Collection

　　撇口，小折沿，弧腹，圈足。内外满釉，外腹壁底部及圈足露胎。口沿内外、碗心及外腹壁底部均饰有弦纹。

（撰稿：王光远、史伟）

景德镇青花海水鱼龙纹碗
Jingdezhen Kiln Blue-and-white Bowl with Fish, Dragon and Waves

2011NASⅥ0106

口径4.4cm　底径6.2cm　高7.5cm

Diameter at Rim 4.4cm　Diameter at Footring 6.2cm　Height 7.5cm

国家文物局水下文化遗产保护中心　藏

National Center of Underwater Cultural Heritage Collection

敞口，斜直腹下弧，圈足。内外满釉，足沿刮釉。青花色泽偏蓝，浓重处发黑。碗心饰海水鱼纹；外腹上、下各饰两周弦纹，腹壁饰双龙赶珠纹，间饰如意云纹，下衬一圈海水纹；圈足外壁两周弦纹，外底饰一方形花押款。

（撰稿：王光远、史伟）

景德镇青花海水鱼龙纹碗
Jingdezhen Kiln Blue-and-white Bowl with Fish, Dragon and Waves

2011NASⅥ0107

口径4.3cm　底径6.0cm　高6.8cm

Diameter at Rim 4.3cm　Diameter at Footring 6.0cm　Height 6.8cm

国家文物局水下文物遗产保护中心　藏

National Center of Underwater Cultural Heritage Collection

　　敞口，斜直腹下弧，圈足。内外满釉，足沿刮釉。青花色泽偏蓝，浓重处发黑。碗心绘海水鱼纹；外腹上、下分别饰两周、一周弦纹，腹壁饰双龙赶珠纹，间饰如意云纹，下衬一圈海水纹；圈足外壁两周弦纹，外底饰一方形花押款。

（撰稿：王光远、史伟）

景德镇青花法螺应龙纹大碗

Jingdezhen Kiln Blue-and-white Large Bowl with Conch and Dragon

2010NANⅣ0103

口径18.4cm　底径6.6cm　高8.5cm

Diameter at Rim 18.4cm　Diameter at Footring 6.6cm　Height 8.5cm

国家文物局水下文化遗产保护中心　藏

National Center of Underwater Cultural Heritage Collection

　　敞口，斜直腹下弧，圈足。内外满釉，足沿刮釉。青花颜色发灰。口沿内侧一周菱形十字锦纹，碗心一周弦纹，内饰法螺纹；外腹上、下各饰一周弦纹，腹壁饰应龙纹，带双翼，间饰卷云纹。圈足外壁两周弦纹，外底饰一方形花押款。

（撰稿：王光远、史伟）

景德镇青花缠枝花卉开光葡萄纹大碗
Jingdezhen Kiln Blue-and-white Large Bowl with Flower Scrolls and Grapevines

2011NANXⅣ0104

口径19.1cm　底径7.0cm　高9.9cm

Diameter at Rim 19.1cm　Diameter at Footring 7.0cm　Height 9.9cm

国家文物局水下文化遗产保护中心　藏

National Center of Underwater Cultural Heritage Collection

敞口，斜直腹下弧，圈足。内外满釉，足沿刮釉。青花色泽偏蓝，浓重处泛黑。内腹壁上下各饰一周弦纹，中饰四开光葡萄纹，碗心一周弦纹内饰蕉叶纹；外腹上、下分别饰两周、一周弦纹，中饰三组缠枝花卉纹；圈足外壁两周弦纹，外底饰两周弦纹，内书"万福攸同"。

（撰稿：王光远、史伟）

景德镇青花高士图"福"款杯
Jingdezhen Kiln Blue-and-white Cup with a Figure and *Fu* Inscription

2010NANV0101
口径6.6　底径2.5cm　高4.1cm
Diameter at Rim 6.6cm　Diameter at Footring 2.5cm　Height 4.1cm
国家文物局水下文化遗产保护中心　藏
National Center of Underwater Cultural Heritage Collection

　　撇口,深腹,斜直腹下弧,圈足。内外满釉,足沿刮釉。青花浅蓝、淡雅。口沿内侧一周粗弦纹,内底一周粗弦纹,内饰坐式人物图;外腹壁上、下一周粗弦纹,中饰高士观景图;圈足外壁一周粗弦纹,外底书"福"字。

(撰稿:王光远、史伟)

景德镇青花高士图"福"款杯
Jingdezhen Kiln Blue-and-white Cup with a Figure and *Fu* Inscription

2010NAC0367

口径6.6cm　底径2.5cm　高4.1cm
Diameter at Rim 6.6cm　Diameter at Footring 2.5cm　Height 4.1cm

国家文物局水下文化遗产保护中心　藏
National Center of Underwater Cultural Heritage Collection

　　撇口，深腹，斜直腹下弧，圈足。内外满釉，足沿刮釉。青花浅蓝、淡雅。口沿内侧一周粗弦纹，内底一周粗弦纹，内饰坐式人物图；外腹壁上、下饰一周粗弦纹，中饰高士观景图；圈足外壁一周粗弦纹，外底书"福"字。

（撰稿：王光远、史伟）

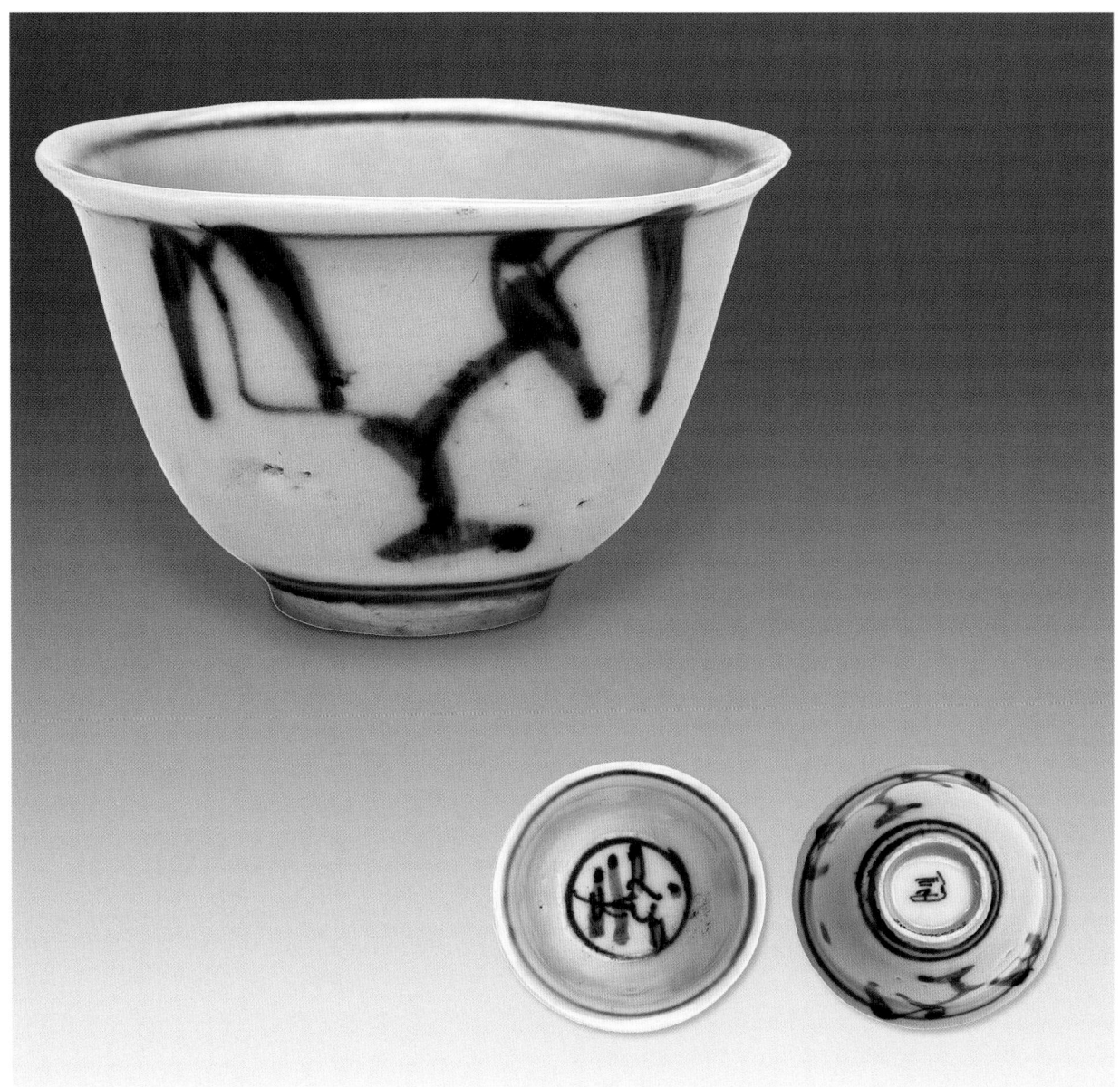

景德镇青花花鸟纹杯
Jingdezhen Kiln Blue-and-white Cup with Flowers and Birds

2010NAC0323

口径6.3cm 底径2.4cm 高4.0cm

Diameter at Rim 6.3cm Diameter at Footring 2.4cm Height 4.0cm

国家文物局水下文化遗产保护中心 藏

National Center of Underwater Cultural Heritage Collection

撇口，深腹，斜直腹下弧，圈足。内外满釉，足沿刮釉。青花浅蓝、淡雅。口沿内侧一周粗弦纹，内底一周粗弦纹，内饰折枝花卉纹；外腹壁上、下一周粗弦纹，中饰两组喜鹊登枝图；圈足外壁一周粗弦纹，外底书"福"字。

（撰稿：王光远、史伟）

景德镇青花兰花纹杯
Jingdezhen Kiln Blue-and-white Cup with Orchids Sprays

2010NANV0102

口径6.0cm　底径2.4cm　高3.7cm

Diameter at Rim 6.0cm　Diameter at Footring 2.4cm　Height 3.7cm

国家文物局水下文化遗产保护中心　藏

National Center of Underwater Cultural Heritage Collection

　　撇口，深腹，斜直腹下弧，圈足。口沿略残。内外满釉，足沿刮釉。青花呈青蓝色。口沿内侧一周粗弦纹，内底一周弦纹，内饰折枝花卉纹；外腹壁上、下一周粗弦纹，中饰两组兰花纹；圈足外壁一周粗弦纹，外底书"福"字。

（撰稿：王光远、史伟）

景德镇青花缠枝牡丹纹"福"款杯
Jingdezhen Kiln Blue-and-white Cup with Peony Scrolls and *Fu* Inscription

2010NAC0369
口径6.6cm 底径2.6cm 高4.1cm
Diameter at Rim 6.6cm   Diameter at Footring 2.6cm   Height 4.1cm
国家文物局水下文化遗产保护中心 藏
National Center of Underwater Cultural Heritage Collection

　　撇口，深腹，斜直腹下弧，圈足。内外满釉，足沿刮釉。青花色泽蓝中带黑。口沿内侧一周粗弦纹，内底一周弦纹，内绘折枝花卉纹；外腹壁上下一周弦纹，中绘缠枝牡丹纹；圈足外壁一周弦纹，外底书"福"字。　　（撰稿：王光远、史伟）

景德镇青花折枝花卉纹"福"款杯
Jingdezhen Kiln Blue-and-white Cup with Flower Sprays and *Fu* Inscription

2010NAC0387

口径6.0cm　底径2.4cm　高3.8cm

Diameter at Rim 6.0cm　Diameter at Footring 2.4cm　Height 3.8cm

国家文物局水下文化遗产保护中心　藏

National Center of Underwater Cultural Heritage Collection

　　撇口，深腹，斜直腹下弧，圈足。内外满釉，足沿刮釉。口沿内侧一周粗弦纹，内底一周粗弦纹，内饰折枝花卉纹；圈足外壁一周粗弦纹，外底书"福"字。

（撰稿：王光远、史伟）

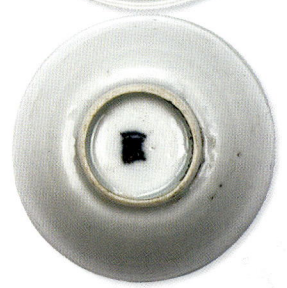

景德镇青花丹凤朝阳图盘

Jingdezhen Kiln Blue-and-white Plate with Phoenix Towards the Sun

2010NAC0362

口径19.5cm　底径9.8cm　高3.2cm

Diameter at Rim 19.5cm　Diameter at Footring 9.8cm　Height 3.2cm

国家文物局水下文化遗产保护中心　藏

National Center of Underwater Cultural Heritage Collection

敞口，宽折沿，弧腹，矮圈足。内外满釉，足沿刮釉。沿面饰五朵杂宝纹，间隔折枝花卉，盘心饰连弧纹边饰条带，内有丹凤朝阳图；口沿外侧及外腹壁各饰花卉纹边饰条带；圈足外壁一周弦纹，外底饰方形印章式款。

（撰稿：王光远、史伟）

景德镇青花树石栏杆纹盘

Jingdezhen Kiln Blue-and-white Plate with Trees, Stone and Railing

2011NASV0106

口径14.8cm　底径7.9cm　高3.1cm

Diameter at Rim 14.8cm　Diameter at Footring 7.9cm　Height 3.1cm

国家文物局水下文化遗产保护中心　藏

National Center of Underwater Cultural Heritage Collection

敞口，窄折沿，浅弧腹，矮圈足。内外满釉，足沿刮釉。青花浓重，泛黑。沿面两周弦纹，盘心两周弦纹内满饰树石栏杆纹；外腹壁绘缠枝花卉；圈足外壁一周弦纹，足沿沾砂。

（撰稿：王光远、史伟）

景德镇青花树石栏杆纹盘

Jingdezhen Kiln Blue-and-white Plate with Trees, Stone and Railing

2011NASV0107

口径14.0cm　底径7.6cm　高1.8cm

Diameter at Rim 14.0cm　Diameter at Footring 7.6cm　Height 1.8cm

国家文物局水下文化遗产保护中心　藏

National Center of Underwater Cultural Heritage Collection

敞口，窄折沿，浅弧腹，矮圈足。内外满釉，足沿刮釉。青花浓重，泛黑。沿面两周弦纹，盘心两周弦纹内满饰树石栏杆纹；外腹壁饰缠枝花卉；圈足外壁一周弦纹。

（撰稿：王光远、史伟）

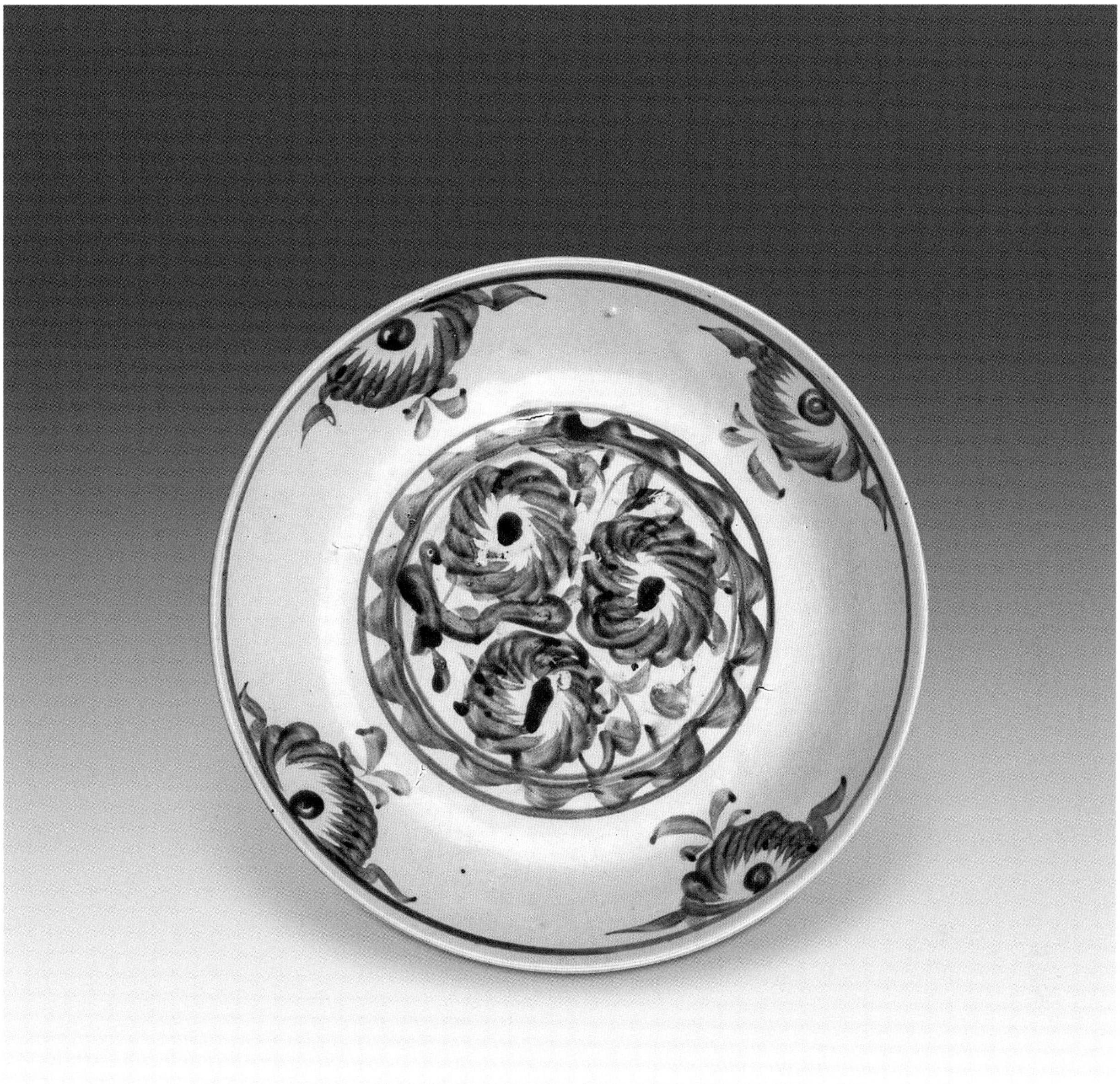

漳州窑青花菊花纹盘

Zhangzhou Kiln Blue-and-white Plate with Chrysanthemum Design

2010NAC0333

口径26.5cm　底径10.5cm　高6.5cm

Diameter at Rim 26.5cm　Diameter at Footring 10.5cm　Height 6.5cm

国家文物局水下文化遗产保护中心　藏

National Center of Underwater Cultural Heritage Collection

侈口，浅弧腹，圈足。内外满釉，足端刮釉。青花色泽灰黑。内腹壁一周弦纹下饰四菊花纹，盘心有三角纹边饰条带，内满饰三朵菊花纹；外腹壁上下、圈足外壁各饰一周弦纹，足端及外底沾砂。　（撰稿：王光远、史伟）

漳州窑青花麒麟纹折沿盘

Zhangzhou Kiln Blue-and-white Plate with Qilin Design and Flat Rim

2010NANⅨ0124

口径26.0cm　底径11.8cm　高6.8cm

Diameter at Rim 26.0cm　Diameter at Footring 11.8cm　Height 6.8cm

国家文物局水下文化遗产保护中心　藏

National Center of Underwater Cultural Heritage Collection

　　敞口，宽折沿，弧腹，圈足。口沿略残。内外满釉。青花色泽灰黑。沿面一周菱形圆点纹条带，盘心有三角纹边饰条带，内饰麒麟纹；外腹壁上、下各饰一周弦纹，足端沾满砂粒。　　　　　　　　　　　　　　　　（撰稿：王光远、史伟）

漳州窑青花缠枝花卉纹玉壶春瓶
Zhangzhou Kiln Blue-and-white Bottle with Flower Scrolls

2011NASⅦ0123
口径5.7cm　底径6.3cm　高14.1cm
Diameter at Rim 5.7cm　Diameter at Footring 6.3cm　Height 14.1cm
国家文物局水下文化遗产保护中心　藏
National Center of Underwater Cultural Heritage Collection

　　喇叭口，束颈，垂弧腹，圈足。口沿略残。青花色泽灰黑。颈部及腹部饰上、中、下三层缠枝花卉纹，间以弦纹；足端露胎，外底施釉不均，有沾砂。

（撰稿：王光远、史伟）

漳州窑青花菊花纹碟
Zhangzhou Kiln Blue-and-white Dish with Chrysanthemum Design

2011NASⅦ0105
口径10.9cm　底径5.0cm　高3.1cm
Diameter at Rim 10.9cm　Diameter at Footring 5.0cm　Height 3.1cm
国家文物局水下文化遗产保护中心　藏
National Center of Underwater Cultural Heritage Collection

敞口，浅弧腹，内底涩圈，圈足。釉不及底。青花色泽灰黑。内外腹壁上、下各饰一周弦纹，碟心饰菊花。

（撰稿：王光远、史伟）

漳州窑青花菊花纹碟
Zhangzhou Kiln Blue-and-white Dish with Chrysanthemum Design

2011NASⅦ0107
口径10.6cm　底径5.3cm　高3.1cm
Diameter at Rim 10.6cm　Diameter at Footring 5.3cm　Height 3.1cm
国家文物局水下文化遗产保护中心　藏
National Center of Underwater Cultural Heritage Collection

　　敞口，浅弧腹，内底涩圈，圈足。釉不及底。青花色泽灰黑。内外腹壁上、下各饰一周弦纹，碟心饰菊花。

（撰稿：王光远、史伟）

漳州窑青花缠枝花卉纹小罐
Zhangzhou Kiln Blue-and-white Small Jar with Flower Scrolls

2010NAN I 0112

口径4.6cm　底径5.9cm　高8.0cm

Diameter at Rim 4.6cm　Diameter at Footring 5.9cm　Height 8.0cm

国家文物局水下文化遗产保护中心　藏

National Center of Underwater Cultural Heritage Collection

敞口，口沿外翻，束颈，溜肩，鼓腹，假圈足。内外满釉，足底露胎。青花色泽灰黑。肩部饰有卷草纹边饰条带，腹部上、下各饰一周弦纹，内饰缠枝花卉纹。

（撰稿：王光远、史伟）

漳州窑青花缠枝花卉纹小罐
Zhangzhou Kiln Blue-and-white Small Jar with Flower Scrolls

2010NAN I 0109

口径4.1cm　底径6.0cm　高37.8cm
Diameter at Rim 4.1cm　Diameter at Footring 6.0cm　Height 37.8cm
国家文物局水下文化遗产保护中心　藏
National Center of Underwater Cultural Heritage Collection

　　敞口，口沿外翻，束颈，溜肩，鼓腹，假圈足。内外满釉，足底露胎。青花色泽灰黑。肩部饰有卷草纹边饰条带，腹部上、下各饰一周弦纹，内饰缠枝花卉纹。

（撰稿：王光远、史伟）

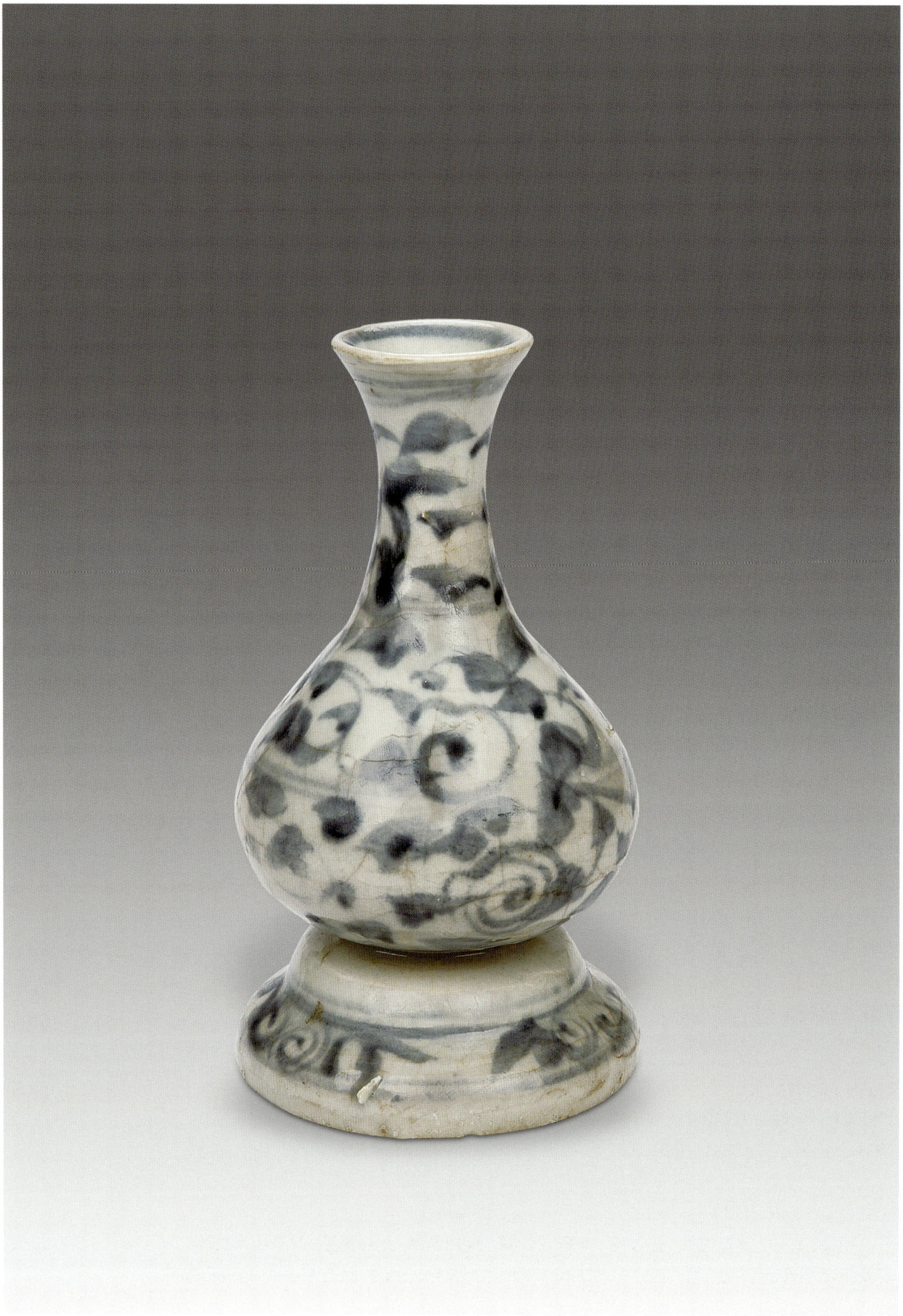

水下考古在中国

102

漳州窑青花缠枝花卉纹净瓶
Zhangzhou Kiln Blue-and-white Bottle with Flower Scrolls

2010NAC0376

口径4.4cm　底径9.2cm　高16.9cm

Diameter at Rim 4.4cm　Diameter at Footring 9.2cm　Height 16.9cm

国家文物局水下文化遗产保护中心　藏

National Center of Underwater Cultural Heritage Collection

敞口，束颈，颈部细长，垂鼓腹，高圈足外撇。内外满釉，足端露胎。青花色泽灰黑。口沿内侧一周弦纹；颈部及腹部满饰缠枝花卉纹；圈足外壁饰有卷草纹边饰条带，圈足内侧有两层台，外底心较平。

（撰稿：王光远、史伟）

景德镇五彩玉兔四开光花卉纹粉盒
Jingdezhen Kiln Famille Verte Cosmetic Box with Rabbit and Flower Sprays

2011NAC0110

口径8.7cm　底径5.7cm　高6.2cm

Diameter at Rim 8.7cm　Diameter at Footring 5.7cm　Height 6.2cm

国家文物局水下文化遗产保护中心　藏

National Center of Underwater Cultural Heritage Collection

　　由盒身和盒盖组成。五彩脱落严重。

　　盒身，子口，弧腹，圈足。内外满釉，足沿刮釉。盒身饰一周缠枝花卉纹。

　　盒盖，芒口，方沿，盖沿斜弧，盖顶较平。盖沿饰四开光花卉纹，盖顶纹样脱落不可辨。

（撰稿：王光远、史伟）

"碗礁I号"清代沉船
Qing Dynasty Shipwreck "Wanjiao I"

"碗礁I号"是一艘清代康熙年间沉船,位于福建平潭碗礁海域,2005年发掘。出水文物共17000余件,大多为景德镇生产的青花瓷器,也有少量的五彩、酱釉瓷器等文物。

The shipwreck "Wanjiao I" dated to Kangxi Reign of Qing Dynasty is located in the Wanjiao Sea of Pingtan in Fujian Province. The ship remains were excavated in 2005. Over 17,000 objects including the Jingdezhen kiln-made blue-and-white porcelains, few Famille Verte wares and brown glazed ceramics were found.

  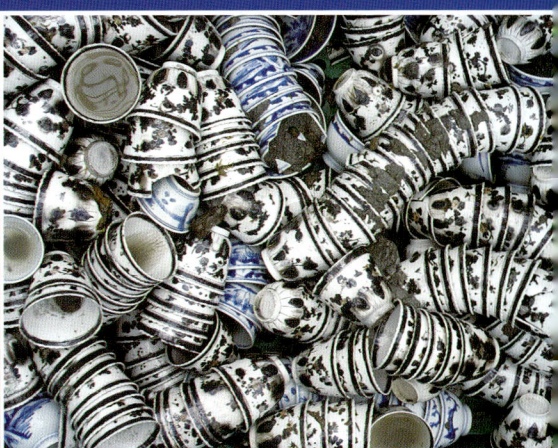

景德镇青花婴戏碗
Jingdezhen Kiln Blue-and-white Bowl with Children Playing Design

J: 02281

口径8.3cm　底径4.0cm　高5.5cm

Diameter at Rim 8.3cm　Diameter at Footring 4.0cm　Height 5.5cm

福州市文物考古工作队　藏

Fuzhou Municipal Institute of Cultural Relics and Archaeology Collection

　　小方唇，敞口，斜直腹下弧，直壁，圈足。内外满釉，足底刮釉。内底饰一戏婴，外腹壁饰婴戏图，外底两周弦纹内饰一方形花押款。

（撰稿：王光远、史伟）

景德镇青花山水碗

Jingdezhen Kiln Blue-and-white Bowl with Landscape Scene

J: 02326

口径8.3cm　底径3.9cm　高5.4cm

Diameter at Rim 8.3cm　Diameter at Footring 3.9cm　Height 5.4cm

福州市文物考古工作队　藏

Fuzhou Municipal Institute of Cultural Relics and Archaeology Collection

　　小方唇，敞口，斜弧腹较深，直壁，圈足。内外满釉，足底刮釉。口沿内侧饰两周弦纹，内底两周弦纹，中饰山水图；口沿外侧两周弦纹，外腹壁饰山水江景图；圈足外壁两周弦纹，外底两周弦纹内饰一方形"卐"字款图案。

（撰稿：王光远、史伟）

景德镇青花山水碗
Jingdezhen Kiln Blue-and-white Bowl with Landscape Scene

J: 02236

口径11.4cm　底径5.0cm　高7.2cm

Diameter at Rim 11.4cm　Diameter at Footring 5.0cm　Height 7.2cm

福州市文物考古工作队　藏

Fuzhou Municipal Institute of Cultural Relics and Archaeology Collection

　　圆唇，敞口，斜弧腹较深，直壁，圈足。内外满釉，足底刮釉。口沿内侧两周弦纹，内底两周弦纹，中饰山水图；口沿外侧两周弦纹，外腹壁饰山水图；圈足外壁两周弦纹，外底两周弦纹，内饰一宝伞图案。

（撰稿：王光远、史伟）

景德镇青花花卉碗
Jingdezhen Kiln Blue-and-white Bowl with Flowers Design

J: 02213

口径11.2cm　底径5.5cm　高5.7cm

Diameter at Rim 11.2cm　Diameter at Footring 5.5cm　Height 5.7cm

福州市文物考古工作队　藏

Fuzhou Municipal Institute of Cultural Relics and Archaeology Collection

　　圆唇，敞口，斜弧腹，直壁，圈足。内外满釉，足底刮釉。口沿内侧饰单圈席纹间饰带，内底心饰菊花纹；口沿外侧单周鱼鳞纹间饰带，外腹壁上部饰四组折枝花卉纹，下部饰十组花卉纹；外底两周弦纹，中饰一宝伞图案。

（撰稿：王光远、史伟）

景德镇青花五开光折枝花卉盘

Jingdezhen Kiln Blue-and-white Plate with Flower Sprays

K: 00032

口径22.0cm　底径12.6cm　高4.0cm

Diameter at Rim 22.0cm　Diameter at Footring 12.6cm　Height 4.0cm

福州市文物考古工作队　藏

Fuzhou Municipal Institute of Cultural Relics and Archaeology Collection

尖唇，撇口，斜弧腹，矮圈足，足壁外斜内直。内外满釉，足底刮釉。口沿内侧五开光折枝花卉边饰，内腹壁饰六组花树纹，盘心两周弦纹内绘七莲花纹；口沿外侧一周弦纹，外腹壁饰三组折枝花卉纹，外底一周弦纹，内饰一方形花押款。

（撰稿：王光远、史伟）

景德镇青花凤穿牡丹碟

Jingdezhen Kiln Blue-and-white Dish with Phoenix amid Peony Scrolls

J: 02455

口径11.8cm　底径5.9cm　高3.2cm

Diameter at Rim 11.8cm　Diameter at Footring 5.9cm　Height 3.2cm

福州市文物考古工作队　藏

Fuzhou Municipal Institute of Cultural Relics and Archaeology Collection

圆唇，撇口，斜弧腹，直壁，圈足。内外满釉，足底刮釉。口沿侧一周弦纹，碟面内底凤穿牡丹纹；外底两周弦纹，内饰一方形花押款。

（撰稿：王光远、史伟）

景德镇青花团菊盘

Jingdezhen Kiln Blue-and-white Plate with Chrysanthemum Posies

L：00010

口径13.7cm　底径7.7cm　高2.1cm

Diameter at Rim 13.7cm　Diameter at Footring 7.7cm　Height 2.1cm

福州市文物考古工作队　藏

Fuzhou Municipal Institute of Cultural Relics and Archaeology Collection

尖唇，撇口，斜弧腹，矮圈足，足壁外斜内直。内外满釉，足底刮釉。口沿内侧饰菊花叶脉纹边饰条带，内腹壁饰四折枝花，内底菊花叶脉纹边饰条带，中饰两周弦纹，内饰团菊；口沿外侧饰菊花叶脉纹边饰条带，外底两周弦纹，内饰叶脉纹。

（撰稿：王光远、史伟）

景德镇青花十六开光五团菊菱口盘
Jingdezhen Kiln Blue-and-white Lobed Plate with Chrysanthemum Posies

K: 00144

口径21.5cm　底径11.0cm　高4.2cm

Diameter at Rim 21.5cm　Diameter at Footring 11.0cm　Height 4.2cm

福州市文物考古工作队　藏

Fuzhou Municipal Institute of Cultural Relics and Archaeology Collection

菱口，斜弧腹，腹壁为十六瓣花形，宽平底，矮圈足，足壁外斜内直。内外满釉，足底刮釉。内腹部十六开光内饰雏菊，内盘心为卷叶地五缠枝菊；外腹亦为十六开光内绘雏菊，外底两周弦纹，内饰折枝菊。　　　　（撰稿：王光远、史伟）

篇章二 展陈文物
Chapter 2 Exhibition Artefacts

117

景德镇青花十六开光洞石花卉菱口盘

Jingdezhen Kiln Blue-and-white Lobed Plate with Stones and Flower Sprays

K: 00131

口径21.4cm 底径11.6cm 高3.9cm

Diameter at Rim 21.4cm Diameter at Footring 11.6cm Height 3.9cm

福州市文物考古工作队 藏

Fuzhou Municipal Institute of Cultural Relics and Archaeology Collection

  菱口，斜弧腹，腹壁为十六瓣菱花形，阔平底，矮圈足，足壁外斜内直。内外满釉，足底刮釉。口沿内外侧饰十六朵连枝十字花卉，腹壁内外十六开光内饰折枝花；盘心为洞石花卉纹；外底青花两周弦纹，内饰杂宝纹。（撰稿：王光远、史伟）

篇章二 展陈文物
Chapter 2 Exhibition Artefacts

119

景德镇青花蓝底冰梅盘

Jingdezhen Kiln Plate with Plum Blossom Reserved in White on Blue Ground

J: 01250

口径16.0cm　底径8.3cm　高2.2cm

Diameter at Rim 16.0cm　Diameter at Footring 8.3cm　Height 2.2cm

福州市文物考古工作队　藏

Fuzhou Municipal Institute of Cultural Relics and Archaeology Collection

　　圆唇，撇口，宽折沿，浅弧腹，阔平底，矮圈足，足壁外斜内直。内外满釉，足底刮釉。沿面、盘心均为冰梅纹，腹部留白；外腹壁饰两组柳枝纹；圈足外壁饰两周弦纹，外底两周弦纹，内饰一杂宝纹。

（撰稿：王光远、史伟）

景德镇青花釉里红梅竹盘

Jingdezhen Kiln Blue-and-white Plate with Plum and Bamboos Design Decorated in Underglazed Blue and Red

J: 00570

口径16.3cm　底径8.9cm　高2.7cm

Diameter at Rim 16.3cm　Diameter at Footring 8.9cm　Height 2.7cm

福州市文物考古工作队　藏

Fuzhou Municipal Institute of Cultural Relics and Archaeology Collection

撇口，小折沿，浅弧腹，宽平底，矮圈足，足壁外斜内直。内外满釉，足底刮釉。盘面饰竹丛枯枝梅花图，花蕊为釉里红彩，花瓣点白色泥浆釉；外腹壁饰四组竹枝，外底两周弦纹，内饰一方形花押款。

（撰稿：王光远、史伟）

景德镇青花高足杯
Jingdezhen Kiln Blue-and-white Stem Cup

J: 02569

口径7.0cm　底径4.8cm　高9.7cm

Diameter at Rim 7.0cm　Diameter at Footring 4.8cm
Height 9.7cm

福州市文物考古工作队　藏
Fuzhou Municipal Institute of Cultural Relics and Archaeology Collection

　　圆唇，芒口，上腹直，下腹内弧，喇叭状高圈足，二层台足底。内外满釉，足底露胎。口沿外侧一周弦纹，外腹壁人物二开光杂宝纹；足柄两周弦纹，上、下各一周圈点纹，足端面两周弦纹，内饰简体蕉叶纹。

（撰稿：王光远、史伟）

景德镇青花菊花深腹杯
Jingdezhen Kiln Blue-and-white Cup with Chrysanthemum Sprays

J: 02522

口径7.0cm　底径3.4cm　高7.5cm
Diameter at Rim 7.0cm　Diameter at Footring 3.4cm　Height 7.5cm
福州市文物考古工作队　藏
Fuzhou Municipal Institute of Cultural Relics and Archaeology Collection

　　圆唇，直口，斜直腹下弧，小平底，矮圈足。内外满釉，足底刮釉。口沿内侧斜线三角形锦地边饰条带；口沿外侧花卉边饰条带；外腹壁上、下两周弦纹，内饰折枝菊，其下菱点纹边饰；圈足外壁一周弦纹。

（撰稿：王光远、史伟）

景德镇五彩杂宝博古盘
Jingdezhen Kiln Famille Verte Plate with Auspicious Treasures

I: 00129

口径13.6cm 底径7.4cm 高2.1cm

Diameter at Rim 13.6cm Diameter at Footring 7.4cm Height 2.1cm

福州市文物考古工作队 藏

Fuzhou Municipal Institute of Cultural Relics and Archaeology Collection

尖唇，撇口，斜弧腹，平底，矮圈足，足壁外斜内直。内外满釉，足底刮釉。口沿内侧五彩宽弦纹，内腹、内底饰五彩杂宝博古图（暗八仙）；外腹三组五彩折枝花；外底青花一周弦纹，内饰折枝杂宝花。五彩呈红、黑褐色。

（撰稿：王光远、史伟）

景德镇五彩八开光折枝花博古盘
Jingdezhen Kiln Famille Verte Plate with Flower Sprays and Vases

J: 02888

口径21.3cm　底径11.6cm　高3.5cm

Diameter at Rim 21.3cm　Diameter at Footring 11.6cm　Height 3.5cm

福州市文物考古工作队　藏

Fuzhou Municipal Institute of Cultural Relics and Archaeology Collection

　　圆唇，撇口，窄沿稍折，斜弧腹，宽平底，矮圈足，足壁外斜内直。内外满釉，足底刮釉。口沿内侧饰五彩半朵花锦地边饰条带，内腹、内底八开光，分别饰五彩折枝花、博古图，盘心一折枝花；外腹三组五彩折枝花；外底青花一周弦纹，内饰折枝杂宝花。五彩呈红、黑褐色。

（撰稿：王光远、史伟）

篇章二 展陈文物
Chapter 2 Exhibition Artefacts

"小白礁I号"清代沉船
Qing Dynasty Shipwreck "Xiaobaijiao I"

"小白礁I号"是一艘清代道光年间沉船，位于浙江宁波象山渔山列岛海域，2008年发现，2009年进行了重点调查与试掘，2012年和2014年分别实施了船载文物与船体发掘。出水遗物1060余件，以底款"嘉庆年制"、"道光年制"青花瓷器为多，兼及五彩瓷、石材、印章、锡器、紫砂壶、西班牙银币和中、日、越南铜钱等。现保护展示于国家水下文化遗产保护宁波基地。

The shipwreck "Xiaobaijiao I" dated to Daoguang Reign of Qing Dynasty is located in the Yushan Archipelago of Ningbo in Zhejiang Province. The ship remains were first discovered in 2008. Archaeological surveys and exploratory were held in 2009. In 2012 and 2014, the shipwreck remains and objects in the cargos have been twice excavated. About 1,060 pieces of objects have been found, the majority of which are blue-and-white porcelains with dated inscription "Jiaqing" or "Daoguang". In addition, the Famille Verte porcelains, stone slabs, seals, tin-works, Yixing clay teapots, Chinese coins and foreign coins from Spain, Japan and Vietnam have also been found. The findings and remains are now housed at the Ningbo Base, National Center of Underwater Cultural Heritage.

景德镇 "嘉庆" 款青花缠枝花卉纹碗
Jingdezhen Kiln Blue-and-white Bowl with Dated Inscription of Jiaqing Reign and Flower Scrolls

2012NXXBW1:3

口径17.7cm　底径8.0cm　高6.9cm

Diameter at Rim 17.7cm　Diameter at Footring 8.0cm　Height 6.9cm

宁波市文物考古研究所　藏

Ningbo Municipal Institute of Cultural Relics and Archaeology Collection

　　敞口，弧腹较深，圈足，制作规整。胎质细白，白釉泛青，釉面莹润，足沿无釉。青花颜色浓重，有晕散效果，纹样线条流畅。口沿内侧饰缠枝花叶纹边饰条带，夹于双弦纹之间，内底心两周内饰缠枝花叶纹；外壁口沿下饰一周弦纹，腹饰缠枝花叶纹，纹样较密，下腹饰一周变体莲纹，间以双弦纹；圈足外壁饰三周弦纹。外底心有青花篆文方形印章式款，可辨"嘉庆"二字，字迹潦草。　　　　　　　　　（撰稿：林国聪、王光远）

景德镇"道光"款青花缠枝花卉纹碗
Jingdezhen Kiln Blue-and-white Bowl with Dated Inscription of Daoguang Reign and Flower Scrolls

2012NXXBW1: 42

口径14.9cm　底径6.3cm　高6.5cm

Diameter at Rim 14.9cm　Diameter at Footring 6.3cm　Height 6.5cm

宁波市文物考古研究所　藏

Ningbo Municipal Institute of Cultural Relics and Archaeology Collection

  敞口，弧腹较深，圈足，制作规整。胎质细白，白釉泛青，釉面莹润，足沿无釉。青花颜色浓重，有晕散效果，纹样线条流畅。口沿内侧饰缠枝花叶纹边饰条带，夹于双弦纹之间，内底心双圈内饰折枝花卉纹；外壁口沿下饰一周弦纹，腹饰缠枝花叶纹，纹样较密，下腹饰一周变体莲纹，间以双弦纹；圈足外壁饰三周弦纹。外底心有青花篆文方形印章式款，可辨"道光"二字，书写草率。

（撰稿：林国聪、王光远）

景德镇青花缠枝花卉纹碗
Jingdezhen Kiln Blue-and-white Bowl with Flower Scrolls

2009NXXBW1: 121

口径9.5cm 底径4.9cm 高4.5cm

Diameter at Rim 9.5cm Diameter at Footring 4.9cm Height 4.5cm

宁波市文物考古研究所 藏

Ningbo Municipal Institute of Cultural Relics and Archaeology Collection

敞口，弧腹较深，圈足，制作规整。胎质细白，白釉泛青，釉面莹润，足沿无釉。青花颜色浓重，有晕散效果，纹样线条流畅。口沿内侧绘缠枝花叶纹边饰条带，夹于双弦纹之间，内底心双圈内饰折枝花卉纹；外壁口沿下饰一周弦纹，腹饰缠枝花叶纹，纹样较密，间以双弦纹；圈足外壁饰三周弦纹。外底心有青花方形印章式款。

（撰稿：林国聪、王光远）

景德镇青花花草纹菱口豆

Jingdezhen Kiln Blue-and-white Lobed Stem Plate with Floral Design

2014NXXBW1: 40

口径11.6cm　底径5.9cm　高5.0cm

Diameter at Rim 11.6cm　Diameter at Footring 5.9cm　Height 5.0cm

宁波市文物考古研究所　藏

Ningbo Municipal Institute of Cultural Relics and Archaeology Collection

　　菱口，折沿，浅弧腹，盘心较平，高圈足外撇。胎质细白，白釉泛青，釉面莹润，足沿无釉。青花色泽鲜艳，有晕散效果。盘沿、内外腹部饰十五组花草纹；内底心饰莲子纹；圈足外壁饰四周弦纹，第二、第三周弦纹之间饰有条带状纹样。

（撰稿：林国聪、王光远）

景德镇青花花草纹菱口豆
Jingdezhen Kiln Blue-and-white Lobed Stem Plate with Floral Design

2014NXXBW1: 41

口径11.0cm　底径6.0cm　高5.0cm

Diameter at Rim 11.0cm　Diameter at Footring 6.0cm　Height 5.0cm

宁波市文物考古研究所　藏

Ningbo Municipal Institute of Cultural Relics and Archaeology Collection

　　菱口，折沿，浅弧腹，盘心较平，高圈足外撇。胎质细白，白釉泛青，釉面莹润，足沿无釉。青花色泽鲜艳，有晕散效果。盘沿、内腹部饰青花地纹，内底心饰花草纹；外腹饰十五组花草纹，其下为放射状直线纹。圈足上下双弦纹，中间饰芭蕉叶纹。

（撰稿：林国聪、王光远）

篇章二 展陈文物
Chapter 2 Exhibition Artefacts

139

景德镇青花灵芝纹盘
Jingdezhen Kiln Blue-and-white Plate with Fungus Design

2012NXXBW1: 81

口径15.1cm　底径9.6cm　高2.7cm

Diameter at Rim 15.1cm　Diameter at Footring 9.6cm　Height 2.7cm

宁波市文物考古研究所　藏

Ningbo Municipal Institute of Cultural Relics and Archaeology Collection

　　敞口，圆唇，斜弧腹，圈足。胎质细白，白釉泛青，釉面莹润，足沿无釉。青花色泽艳丽。内腹满饰灵芝纹；内底边缘饰一周葵纹，底心饰一朵折枝花卉；外腹饰三朵折枝花卉；外底饰双弦纹，中心绘青花方形印章式款。　　（撰稿：林国聪、王光远）

景德镇青花菊瓣纹"福"款盘

Jingdezhen Kiln Blue-and-white Plate with Chrysanthemum Petals and *Fu* Inscription

2012NXXBW1∶78

口径16.0cm　底径9.8cm　高3.3cm

Diameter at Rim 16.0cm　Diameter at Footring 9.8cm　Height 3.3cm

宁波市文物考古研究所　藏

Ningbo Municipal Institute of Cultural Relics and Archaeology Collection

敞口，圆唇，斜弧腹，圈足。内底涩圈，外底心有脐突。胎灰白，质较细。釉色青白，釉层较厚，外足端刮釉。青花色泽泛灰。内腹绘一周菊瓣纹，夹于双弦纹之间；内底心书"福"字，边饰一圆圈纹；外腹口沿下饰一周弦纹，圈足外壁饰两周弦纹。

（撰稿：林国聪、王光远）

景德镇青花花卉纹碟

Jingdezhen Kiln Blue-and-white Dish with Flowers Design

2008NXXBW1: 7

口径8.6cm 底径4.3cm 高2.5cm

Diameter at Rim 8.6cm Diameter at Footring 4.3cm Height 2.5cm

宁波市文物考古研究所 藏

Ningbo Municipal Institute of Cultural Relics and Archaeology Collection

　　侈口，斜弧腹，圈足，制作规整。胎质细白，白釉泛青，釉面莹润，足沿无釉。青花颜色浓重，晕散明显，纹样线条流畅。口沿外侧绘双弦纹，外壁绘缠枝花卉纹，圈足外壁饰一周弦纹。内壁饰青花地纹，内底满饰缠枝花叶纹，边缘饰两周弦纹。

（撰稿：林国聪、王光远）

景德镇青花缠枝花草纹灯盏
Jingdezhen Kiln Blue-and-white Lamp with Floral Scrolls

2008NXXBW1: 16

灯盘口径5.1cm　底径4.1cm　灯台口径10.5cm　底径6.8cm　通高10.5cm

Upper Disc: Upper Diameter 5.1cm Lower Diameter 4.1cm

Lower Disc: Upper Diameter 10.5cm Lower Diameter 6.8cm

Overall Height 10.5cm

宁波市文物考古研究所　藏

Ningbo Municipal Institute of Cultural Relics and Archaeology Collection

灯盘撇口，折腹，盘心平。灯柱呈细长柱状，上细，下粗，中空，把残。灯台呈盘状，侈口，盘心平，矮圈足。胎质细白，白釉泛青，釉面莹润，外底无釉。青花色泽明艳，纹样线条流畅。灯盘、灯台饰卷云纹、卷草纹、花草纹，灯柱上饰缠枝花草纹，下饰蕉叶纹。　　　　（撰稿：林国聪、王光远）

篇章二 展陈文物
Chapter 2 Exhibition Artefacts

景德镇青花花卉纹杯

Jingdezhen Kiln Blue-and-white Cup with Flowers Design

2009NXXBW1: 91

口径6.7cm　底径3.5cm　高3.2cm

Diameter at Rim 6.7cm　Diameter at Footring 3.5cm
Height 3.2cm

宁波市文物考古研究所 藏

Ningbo Municipal Institute of Cultural Relics and Archaeology Collection

　　敞口，弧腹较深，圈足，制作规整。胎质细白，白釉泛青，釉面莹润，足沿无釉。青花颜色浓重，有晕散效果，纹样线条流畅。口沿内侧绘缠枝花叶纹边饰条带，夹于双弦纹之间，内底心双圈内饰折枝花卉纹；外壁口沿下饰一周弦纹，腹饰缠枝花叶纹，纹样较密，间以双弦纹；圈足外壁饰一周弦纹。外底心有青花方形印章式款。

（撰稿：林国聪、王光远）

景德镇青花花草纹勺
Jingdezhen Kiln Blue-and-white Spoon with Floral Design

2014NXXBW1: 7

长11.5cm　宽5.2cm　高4.3cm

Length 11.5cm　Width 5.2cm　Height 4.3cm

宁波市文物考古研究所　藏

Ningbo Municipal Institute of Cultural Relics and Archaeology Collection

　　敞口，直柄，平底内凹。胎质细白，白釉泛青，釉面莹润，足底刮釉。青花颜色浓重，晕散明显，纹样线条流畅。勺内侧饰缠枝花草纹，外底心有青花方形印章式款。

（撰稿：林国聪、王光远）

景德镇五彩盖罐
Jingdezhen Kiln Famille Verte Jar

2009NXXBW1：474（盖）　2009NXXBW1：475（罐）

盖　口径12.1cm　沿径15.3cm　高7.5cm

罐　口径14.4cm　底径8.7cm　高10.3cm

通高17.9cm

Lid: Inner Diameter 12.1cm　Outer Diameter 15.3cm　Height 7.5cm

Jar: Diameter at Rim 14.4cm　Diameter at Footring 8.7cm　Height 10.3cm

Overall Height 17.9cm

宁波市文物考古研究所　藏

Ningbo Municipal Institute of Cultural Relics and Archaeology Collection

　　盖子口，盖沿外折，盖面隆起，双层塔式宝珠钮。白胎细腻，盖内沿无釉。盖面纹饰图案模糊不清，可见黑色斑块。器表有贝类附着物。

　　罐芒口，母口，斜直腹微弧，圈足。白胎细腻，足沿内外刮削无釉。罐身口沿下和腹底部饰一周连珠纹，外腹壁密布绿色图案或残迹。器表有贝类附着物。

（撰稿：林国聪、王光远）

篇章二 展陈文物
Chapter 2 Exhibition Artefacts

149

紫砂壶
Yixing Clay Teapot

2012NXXBW1: 91

口径6.2cm 底径6.9cm 高4.4cm

Diameter at Rim 6.2cm　Diameter at Footring 6.9cm　Height 4.4cm

宁波市文物考古研究所 藏

Ningbo Municipal Institute of Cultural Relics and Archaeology Collection

　　红胎，胎质细腻。敛口，方沿，折弧腹，平底微内凹，有流，有把，盖失。素面无纹。底款"二水中分白鹭洲孟臣制"。　　　　（撰稿：林国聪、王光远）

紫砂罐
Yixing Clay Jar

2014NXXBW1: 60

口径2.5cm　底径5.0cm　高6.5cm

Diameter at Rim 2.5cm　Diameter at Footring 5.0cm　Height 6.5cm

宁波市文物考古研究所　藏

Ningbo Municipal Institute of Cultural Relics and Archaeology Collection

　　红胎，胎质细腻。敛口，方沿，短颈，溜肩，鼓腹，圈足，平底。素面无纹。　　　　（撰稿：林国聪、王光远）

酱釉陶壶
Brown Glazed Ewer

2009NXXBW1: 31

口径8.0cm 底径10.5cm 高16.3cm

Diameter at Rim 8.0cm Diameter at Footring 10.5cm Height 16.3cm

宁波市文物考古研究所 藏

Ningbo Municipal Institute of Cultural Relics and Archaeology Collection

敛口，圆唇，束颈，斜弧腹，平底内凹，流上部与颈肩有粘接。酱黑釉，内口沿有釉，内腹无釉。

（撰稿：林国聪、王光远）

"源合盛记"印章
Seal with *Yuanheshengji* Inscription

2008NXXBW1: 12

边长2.7cm 高3.1cm

Length 2.7cm Width 2.7cm Height 3.1cm

宁波市文物考古研究所 藏

Ningbo Municipal Institute of Cultural Relics and Archaeology Collection

叶腊石，正四棱柱状。印面正方形，双边框。阳刻楷体反纹"源合盛记"；顶面刻"上"字，与底面印文字方向相同。

（撰稿：林国聪、王光远）

西班牙银币
Spanish Silver Coin

2008NXXBW1: 11
直径3.9cm　厚0.2cm
Diameter 3.9cm　Thickness 0.2cm
宁波市文物考古研究所　藏
Ningbo Municipal Institute of Cultural Relics and Archaeology Collection

　　银质，圆形，边缘压花，表面有磨损，图案模糊。正面图案、印文模糊不识，应为头像和铸造年代；背面是王冠、盾徽，两边双柱，周围镌刻西班牙文"HISPAN.ETIND.REX.M.8R.F.M"，并戳印有不同样式的字符。

（撰稿：林国聪、王光远）

测深铅锤
Sounding Lead

2014NXXBW1:65
底径4.0cm　高9.3cm
Diameter at bottom 4.0cm　Height 9.3cm
宁波市文物考古研究所　藏
Ningbo Municipal Institute of Cultural Relics and Archaeology Collection

　　铅锡合金。圆锥状，上细下粗，顶端残，近顶端处有一圆孔，用于穿绳。器表锈蚀，有贝类附着物。用于行船测量水深。　　　　　　　　　（撰稿：林国聪、王光远）

中山舰
Zhongshan Warship

　　"中山舰"是我国近现代史上的一代名舰,1908年由清政府向日本订购,原名"永丰舰",其后经历了护国运动、护法动动、孙中山广州蒙难事件、抗日战争等重大历史事件。1938年被日军炸沉于湖北武汉金口长江水域。

　　"中山舰"水下考古是我国内水首个大型水下文化遗产保护项目。1986年湖北省提出打捞保护动议,随后经国家文物局批准,于1997年被整体打捞出水。2001年"中山舰"舰体修复保护工程竣工,2008年修复后的"中山舰"被运回武汉市江夏区金口镇。现存湖北武汉中山舰博物馆。

The Zhongshan Warship, or called Yongfeng, is one of the most famous warships in early modern Chinese history. It was built in Japan and sold to the Qing China in 1908. It experienced many different historical events such as National Protection War, Constitutional Protection Movement, the Zhongshan Warship Incident and the second Sino-Japanese War. It was sunk by the Japanese army at Yangtze River of Jinkou, Wuhan, Hubei Province in 1938.

The Zhongshan Warship Underwater Archaeology Project is the first inland water project of China's underwater cultural heritage reservation. In 1986, this project has been proposed by the Hubei Provincial Government and has been issued by the State Administration of Cultural Heritage. In 1997, the ship remains have been salvaged and the boat was reconstructed in 2001. The re-decorated warship voyaged back to the Jinkou County of the Jiangxia district of Wuhan City in 2008 and is now parking at the Zhongshan Warship Museum in Wuhan City of Hubei Province.

"中山"木牌

Wooden Badge with Inscription *Zhongshan*

长3.8cm　宽0.5cm　厚5.8cm
Length 3.8cm　Width 0.5cm　Thickness 5.8cm
中山舰博物馆　藏
Zhongshan Warship Museum Collection

　　木质。碑状。正面刻有"中山"二字。应为"永丰舰"易名为"中山舰"之后舰上日常使用之物。

（撰稿：胡珏珩）

驳壳手枪
Mauser Pistol

Z: 3489

长25.6cm 宽15.5cm 厚2.8cm

Length 25.6cm Width 15.5cm Thickness 2.8cm

中山舰博物馆 藏

Zhongshan Warship Museum Collection

铁质，握把木质部分已不存，其他部件基本完整。

驳壳枪，正式名称为毛瑟军用手枪（Mauser Military Pistol）。由于其枪套是一个木盒，因此在中国也称匣子枪或盒子炮。

（撰稿：胡珏珩）

七九式步枪
79 Rifle

Z: 3651

长126.0cm　宽20.5cm　厚9.0cm

Length 126.0cm　Width 20.5cm　Thickness 9.0cm

中山舰博物馆　藏

Zhongshan Warship Museum Collection

铁质，枪杆处的木质部分已腐蚀脱落，其他部分基本完整。

中山舰上出水了数十杆七九式步枪，应为第一次国共合作时期北伐战争时使用的枪械，产地与同时出水的水冷式重机枪一样，都来自广东兵工厂。

（撰稿：胡珏珩）

七九式步枪刺刀
79 Rifle Bayonet

Z: 3530
长40.8cm　宽7.7cm　高2.6cm
Length 40.8cm　Width 7.7cm　Height 2.6cm
中山舰博物馆　藏
Zhongshan Warship Museum Collection

铁质刀身，剑形状，配有刀鞘。刀柄处的木质部分已腐蚀严重。该刺刀是装于七九式步枪前端的刺杀兵器，也能从步枪上取下装入刀鞘携行。

（撰稿：胡珏珩）

扳手
Wrench

长28.3cm　宽6.4cm　厚1.3cm
Length 28.3cm　Width 6.4cm　Thickness 1.3cm
中山舰博物馆　藏
Zhongshan Warship Museum Collection

　　铁质，锈蚀严重，基本完整。单头扳手。中山舰上出水了大量的五金工具，应为军舰日常维护用具。

（撰稿：胡珏珩）

炮弹壳
Artillery Shell

Z：3756

底径7.6cm　口径4.5cm　高41.0cm

Diameter at Footring 7.6cm　Diameter at Rim 4.5cm　Height 41.0cm

中山舰博物馆　藏

Zhongshan Warship Museum Collection

　　铜质，有锈迹。直筒状。中山舰上出水数百枚此种炮弹壳。（撰稿：胡珏珩）

弹壳笔筒
Brush Pot Made of Artillery Shell

Z: 3234

口径4.0cm 底径4.8cm 高16.0cm

Diameter at Rim 4.0cm   Diameter at Footring 4.8cm   Height 16.0cm

中山舰博物馆 藏

Zhongshan Warship Museum Collection

铜质，有锈迹。直筒状，已制作成笔筒。 （撰稿：胡珏珩）

砚台
Inkstone

Z: 1901

长8.5cm　宽8.5cm　厚2.4cm

Length 8.5cm　Width 8.5cm　Thickness 2.4cm

中山舰博物馆　藏

Zhongshan Warship Museum Collection

　　石质。方形。砚盖母口，有凸起边框；砚身子口，砚面圆形、直壁较深；外底内凹。通体青黑，光素无纹。中山舰出水了数十件此类砚台，应为舰上将士日常使用之物。

（撰稿：胡珏珩）

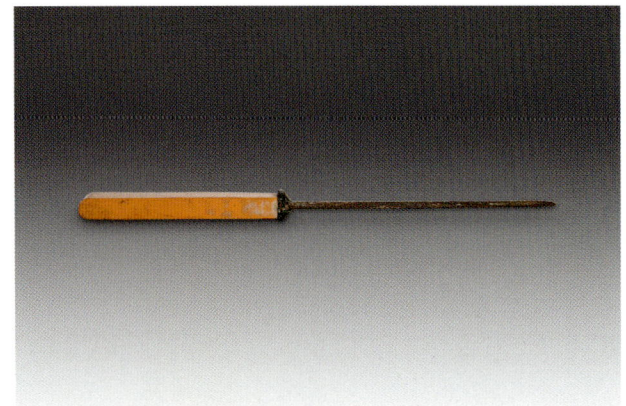

开信刀
Letter Opener

Z: 1476

长19.8cm　宽2.0cm　厚1.1cm

Length 19.8cm　Width 2.0cm　Thickness 1.1cm

中山舰博物馆　藏

Zhongshan Warship Museum Collection

铁质刀体，锈蚀严重；刀柄为塑料，基本完整。　（撰稿：胡珏珩）

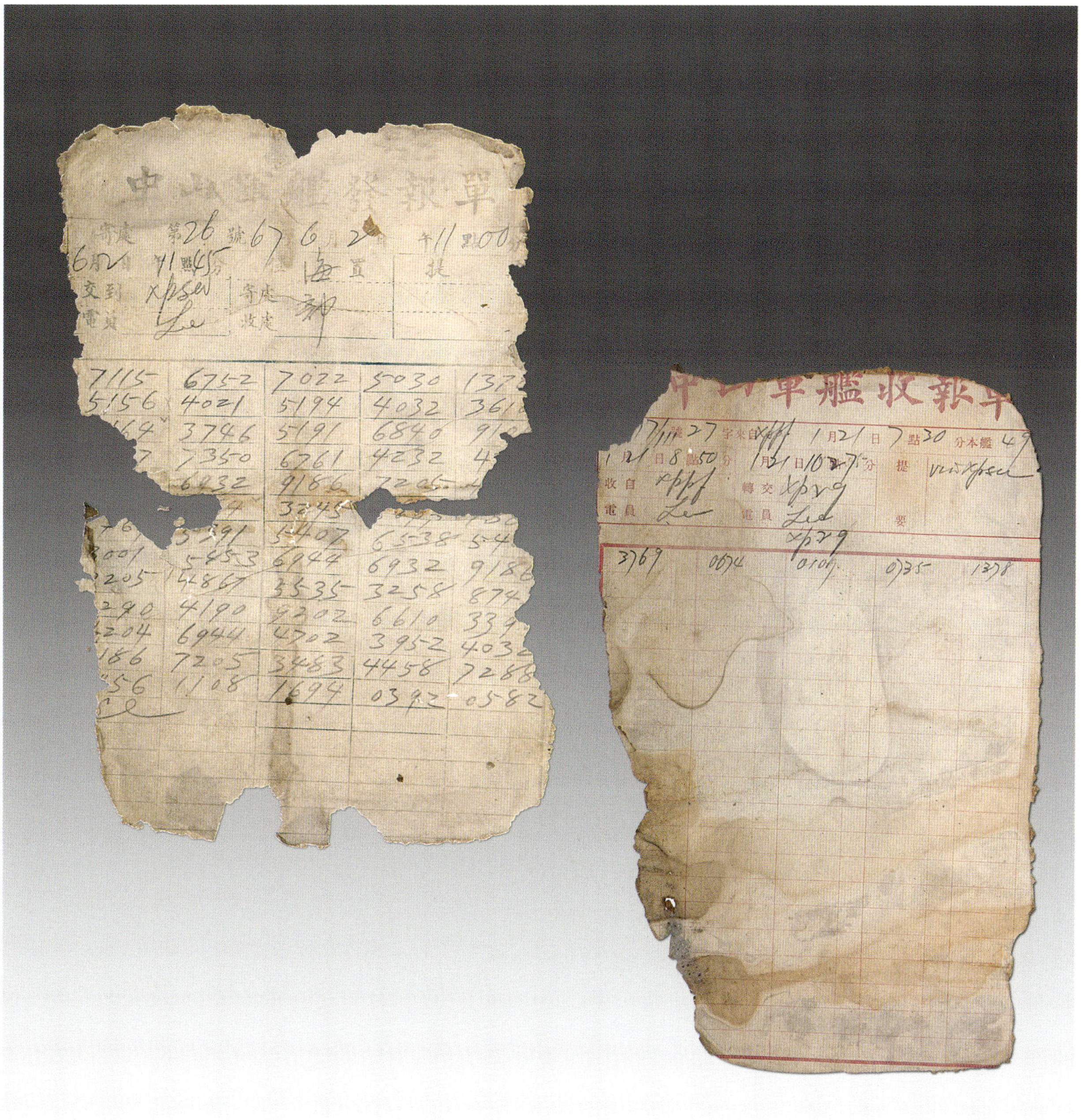

中山军舰电报稿
Telegram Manuscript

FB527（发报单）

长34.5cm　宽27.3cm（装裱后）

Length 34.5cm　Width 27.3cm

中山舰博物馆　藏

Zhongshan Warship Museum Collection

SB313（收报单）

长33.5cm　宽23.5cm（装裱后）

Length 33.5cm　Width 23.5cm

中山舰博物馆　藏

Zhongshan Warship Museum Collection

　　纸质。边缘部分腐蚀严重。发报单蓝色底纹，收报单红色底纹，上端印文清晰，稿文用铅笔书写，字迹清晰。

　　目前，已破译出350余份中山舰电报稿，主要内容涉及中山舰的日常巡防、编训情况、人员升迁与调动、设备维护与添置以及与外国军舰的交往等情况。

（撰稿：胡珏珩）

铜纽扣
Copper Button

直径2.2cm　厚1.2cm

Diameter 2.2cm　Thickness 1.2cm

中山舰博物馆　藏

Zhongshan Warship Museum Collection

　　铜质。圆形。纽面为凸起的国民党党徽和铁锚组合图案，周边饰一圈绳纹；纽背有一穿线圆环，圆环两边各有一孔。应为海军军服纽扣。　　　　（撰稿：胡珏珩）

刮胡刀
Shaver

Z：2681
长4.0cm　宽2.4cm　高8.2cm
Length 4.0cm　Width 2.4cm　Height 8.2cm
中山舰博物馆　藏
Zhongshan Warship Museum Collection

金属材质。由刀片和锄形刀架组成。为安全刮胡刀。

安全刮胡刀是19世纪后期法国人雅克佩雷发明的，灵感来自于木匠制造的飞机机翼，既装置了使用便利的锋利刀片，又能够保护使用者的皮肤安全。安全刮胡刀于1875年上市，有"不会被割喉咙"的美誉。

（撰稿：胡珏珩）

军用水壶
Canteen

Z:1395

长12.6cm 宽6.0cm 高19.4cm

Length 12.6cm   Width 6.0cm   Height 19.4cm

中山舰博物馆 藏

Zhongshan Warship Museum Collection

铝合金材质。壶身有磨损，有锈迹，壶塞不存。 （撰稿：胡珏珩）

"汉口赞誉"汽水瓶

Soda Pop Bottle with Inscription *Hankouzanyu*

Z：2420

口径2.3cm　底径4.5cm　高21.7cm

Diameter at Rim 2.3cm　Diameter at Footring 4.5cm　Height 21.7cm

中山舰博物馆　藏

Zhongshan Warship Museum Collection

　　玻璃质。圆唇，直口，束沿，长颈，弧腹，平底。外腹一面阳文"汉口赞誉汽水厂"，另一面阳书一圈"HANKOWDISPENSARYLTO·WOKNAH·"字样，内有其标识图案。

　　汉口赞誉汽水厂是武汉冷饮行业史上第一家采用机器制作汽水的冷饮厂。其前身是法国商人纳加利于1911年在汉口法租界海寿街（现车站路附近）开办的一家小规模的、人工生产碳酸汽水的车间。1918年英商开办的"赞誉药房"收购了这家人工汽水车间，取名"汉口赞誉汽水厂"，并加以扩建，添置新式设备，成为汉口第一家机器制作汽水的冷饮厂。

（撰稿：胡珏珩）

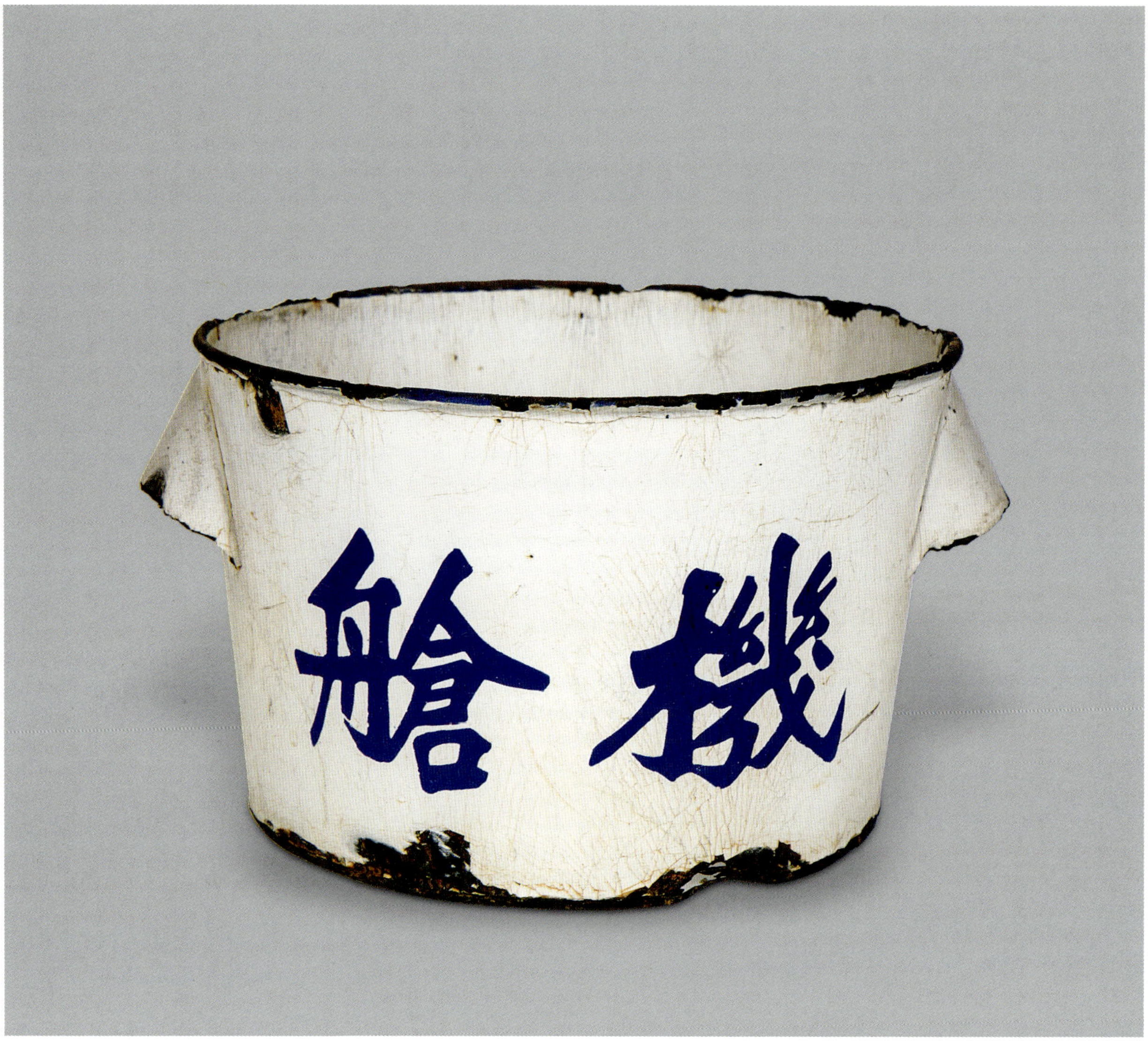

"机舱"双耳搪瓷缸

Two-handle Enamel Mug with Inscription *Jicang*

口径17.3cm 底径14.7cm 高11.3cm

Diameter at Rim 17.3cm Diameter at Footring 14.7cm Height 11.3cm

中山舰博物馆 藏

Zhongshan Warship Museum Collection

  铁质，薄胎。直口，双耳，斜直腹下收，底不存。内外白色瓷釉，口沿唇部钴锈蚀严重，可见蓝色瓷釉。外腹壁书"机舱"二字，繁体，钴蓝色。应为舰上将士日常生活用品。

（撰稿：胡珏珩）

"平海"搪瓷脸盆

Enamel Washbasin with Inscription *Pinghai*

Z: 2962

口径17.3cm 底径22.0cm 高11.3cm

Diameter at Rim 17.3cm Diameter at Footring 22.0cm Height 11.3cm

中山舰博物馆 藏

Zhongshan Warship Museum Collection

铁质，薄胎。直口，宽折沿，斜直腹，平底。口沿及底残。内外白色瓷釉，口沿唇部钴蓝色瓷釉。内底书"平海"二字，篆体，钴蓝色；外腹壁书单字"性"，魏碑体，钴蓝色；外底有"立鹤"图案，下书"中华珐琅厂立鹤牌面盆"。

"平海"号为国民政府海军部仿"宁海"号建造的一艘轻巡洋舰，由日本提供零组件，江南造船厂承造，是中国抗战时期海军"装备最强"的一艘军舰。

中华珐琅厂是嘉定著名实业家方剑阁于1921年创办的，生产搪瓷器皿，注册"立鹤"商标。

中山舰上出水了多件有"平海"字样的搪瓷生活用品，据此推测中山舰上可能有曾在平海舰服役过的将士。

（撰稿：胡珏珩）

手电筒
Torch

Z: 1861

顶径5.6cm 底径4.1cm 高17.8cm

Diameter at Rim 5.6cm   Diameter at Footring 4.1cm   Height 17.8cm

中山舰博物馆 藏

Zhongshan Warship Museum Collection

  铜质。筒身基本完整，玻璃灯罩和灯泡已不存。底部有"无畏"字样商标，"大无畏牌"、"汇明"等字样。

  该手电筒生产厂商是近代著名实业家丁熊照先生，他于1925年创立的上海汇明电筒电池厂是我国专业电筒、电池生产厂的元老。"大无畏牌"产品的诞生，一举打破洋货洋牌长期垄断我国电筒、电池市场的不利局面。

  1940年出版的《上海汇明电筒电池制造厂样本》中有一段记载厂史的文字："回溯从前草创之时，技术困难，环境恶劣，组织未备，人事不良。种种阻挠，均以百折不挠之大无畏精神予以克服，故本厂主要产品，均用大无畏为商标。"

（撰稿：胡珏珩）

壁式可转动挂衣杆
Wall Mount Clothes Hanger

长41.8cm　宽11.2cm　厚2.5cm
Length 41.8cm　Width 11.2cm　Thickness 2.5cm

中山舰博物馆　藏
Zhongshan Warship Museum Collection

　　铜质。蝴蝶状底座，四角有四个圆孔，用于固定螺丝；锯齿状挂杆，与底座连接，可左右转动。

（撰稿：胡珏珩）

手提灯
Portable Lamp

Z：2552

长13.8cm 宽11.0cm 高37.5cm

Length 13.8cm Width 11.0cm Height 37.5cm

中山舰博物馆 藏

Zhongshan Warship Museum Collection

铜质构架，把手外套木柄已残，玻璃灯罩，未装灯泡。长勾状提手，灯架瘦长，有四立足。

（撰稿：胡珏珩）

后　记

2014年10月16日，国家水下文化遗产保护宁波基地正式建成投用，"水下考古在中国"专题陈列同步对外开放。值此宁波基地建成投用、专题陈列对外开放周年将届之际，这本《水下考古在中国——专题陈列图录》的付梓出版，可以说是为基地的落成和陈列的开展献上的最有纪念意义的礼物之一。

"水下考古在中国"陈列大纲由宁波市文物考古研究所（国家水下文化遗产保护宁波基地）负责编制。王结华主持展陈策划并负责大纲的统稿工作；王力军、林国聪等共同负责大纲的编写工作；王光远、金涛、张华琴，以及国家文物局水下文化遗产保护中心的李滨、邓启江、孟原召、梁国庆等负责资料的收集整理；宁波中国港口博物馆的吴凤、王文武等为陈列的设计布展提供了全程协助。对以上诸位的努力，在此一并致谢。

《水下考古在中国——专题陈列图录》由王结华负责整体策划和全文统稿；概述、后记由王结华、王力军共同撰写；林国聪负责协调图片拍摄、文稿校对及编辑出版工作；王光远、金涛、史伟、侯鲜婷等负责资料整理与协助拍摄工作；周昳恒、洪欣担纲英文翻译；照片由冯毅、孙臣、黄欢、李朱佳拍摄。

中国文化遗产研究院刘曙光院长，国家文物局水下文化遗产保护中心柴晓明主任、张威书记、水下考古研究所姜波所长、办公室赵嘉斌主任，宁波市文化广电新闻出版局赵惠峰局长、舒月明副局长、徐建成处长等领导对本图录的出版给予了大力支持；宁波出版社编辑卓挺亚、王晓君等人为本图录的出版付出了辛勤劳动。值此书稿付梓之际，谨向他们致以衷心的谢意。

由于编者水平有限，本图录编著过程中出现的疏漏与错误在所难免，尚祈各位读者见谅并指正。

编者
2015年8月

Postscript

In 16th October, 2014, Ningbo Base, National Center of Underwater Cultural Heritage and *Underwater Archaeology in China* Exhibition opened to the public at the same time. Today, the publication of *The Collection of Underwater Archaeology in China Exhibition* could be regarded as one of the most significant anniversary gifts to the base and the exhibition.

The display outline of the *Underwater Archaeology in China* Exhibition is edited by the Ningbo Municipal Institute of Cultural Relics and Archaeology (Ningbo Base, National Center of Underwater Cultural Heritage). Here we would like to send out gratitude to the staff who have made their efforts to the display and the outline: Wang Jiehua is in charge of the display and is the chief editor of the outline; Wang Lijun and Lin Guocong are the co-writers of the outline; Wang Guangyuan, Jin Tao, Zhang Huaqin and Li Bin, Deng Qijiang, Meng Yuanzhao, Liang Guoqing from National Center of Underwater Cultural Heritage are responsible for the data collecting; Wu Feng, Wang Wenwu from China Port Museum kindly have offered help to the display design.

The book *The Collection of the Exhibition of Underwater Archaeology in China* is chiefly edited by Wang Jiehua. The introduction and the postscript of the book are written by Wang Jiehua and Wang Lijun. Lin Guocong is in charge of coordinating the photography, proofreading and publication. Wang Guangyuan, Jin Tao, Shi Wei and Hou Xianting are responsible for the data organizing the photography assisting. The book is translated by Zhou Yiheng and Hong Xin. The photos are shot by Feng Yi, Sun Cheng, Huang Huan and Li Zhujia.

On the occasion of the completion of this book, we'd like to express our sincere appreciation to Liu Shuguang, Head of Chinese Academy of Cultural Heritage ; Chai Xiaoming, Director of National Center of Underwater Cultural Heritage; Zhang Wei, Party Branch Secretary of National Center of Underwater Cultural Heritage; Jiang Bo, Director of Underwater Archaeology Department of National Center of Underwater Cultural Heritage; Zhao Jiabin, Director of the office of National Center of Underwater Cultural Heritage ; Zhao Huifeng, General Director of Culture, Radio, Television, Press and Publication Bureau of Ningbo; ShuYueming, Deputy General Director of Culture, Radio, Television, Press and Publication Bureau of Ningbo; XuJiancheng , Director of Cultural Relics and Museum Department of Culture, Radio, Television, Press and Publication Bureau of Ningbo and ZhuoTingya, Wang Xiaojun, the editor from Ningbo Publishing House .

Confined to the ability of the editors, there are inevitable mistakes and flaws in this book. Please feel free to correct us.

Editor

August 2015

图书在版编目（CIP）数据

水下考古在中国：专题陈列图录 / 宁波市文物考古研究所，宁波中国港口博物馆，国家文物局水下文化遗产保护中心编著 . — 宁波：宁波出版社，2015.10

ISBN 978-7-5526-2258-4

Ⅰ. ①水… Ⅱ. ①宁… ②宁… ③国… Ⅲ. ①考古技术—水下技术—中国—图录 Ⅳ. ① K870.2

中国版本图书馆 CIP 数据核字（2015）第 224945 号

水下考古在中国
专题陈列图录

编　　著	宁波市文物考古研究所
	宁波中国港口博物馆
	国家文物局水下文化遗产保护中心

出版发行	宁波出版社（宁波市甬江大道 1 号宁波书城 8 号楼 6 楼　315040）
网　　址	http://www.nbcbs.com
责任编辑	卓挺亚
责任校对	虞姬颖
责任审读	王　丹
制　　版	浙江新华图文制作有限公司
印　　刷	浙江新华数码印务有限公司
开　　本	889 毫米 ×1194 毫米　1 / 16
印　　张	12
字　　数	100 千
版　　次	2015 年 10 月第 1 版
印　　次	2015 年 10 月第 1 次印刷
书　　号	ISBN 978-7-5526-2258-4
定　　价	268.00 元

如发现缺页或倒装，影响阅读，请与承印厂联系调换。电话：0571-85155604